The Wild Side

Crime and Punishment

The Wild Side
Crime and Punishment

Henry Billings
Melissa Billings

JAMESTOWN PUBLISHERS

a division of NTC/CONTEMPORARY PUBLISHING GROUP
Lincolnwood, Illinois USA

ISBN 0–8092-9518-0

Published by Jamestown Publishers,
a division of NTC/Contemporary Publishing Group, Inc.
4255 West Touhy Avenue,
Lincolnwood (Chicago), Illinois 60712-1975, U.S.A.

4 5 6 7 8 9 10 11 12 113/055 09 08 07 06 05 04

CONTENTS

UNIT THREE

To the Student

We hear about crimes on the news every day. We seem to be hungry for all the details, we formulate our own opinions on the guilt or innocence of the accused, and often we vehemently agree or disagree with the sentence that is given to offenders. Although we deplore crime, we are also intrigued by it. In *Crime and Punishment*, students will take a close look at some of the most controversial and memorable crimes and criminals of the past two centuries. In some articles, students will have an opportunity to see the early, private lives that led to the public lives of crime. In others, they will read about the personalities and planning behind the crime. Still others raise questions that may never be answered fully. These high-interest articles capitalize on students' natural fascination with crime and punishment.

As you read and enjoy the 15 articles in this book, you will be developing your reading skills. If you complete all the lessons in this book, you will surely increase your reading speed and improve your reading comprehension and critical thinking skills. Also, because these exercises include items of the types often found on state and national tests, learning how to complete them will prepare you for tests you may have to take in the future.

How to Use This Book

About the Book.   *Crime and Punishment* contains three units, each of which includes five lessons. Each lesson begins with an article about an unusual subject or event. The article is followed by a group of four reading comprehension exercises and three critical thinking exercises. The reading comprehension exercises will help you understand the article. The critical thinking exercises will help you think about what you have read and how it relates to your own experience.

   At the end of each lesson, you will also have the opportunity to give your personal response to some aspect of the article and then to assess how well you understood what you read.

The Sample Lesson.   Working through the sample lesson, the first lesson in the book, with your class or group will demonstrate how a lesson is organized. The sample lesson explains how to complete the exercises and score your answers. The correct answers for the sample exercises and sample scores are printed in lighter type. In some cases, explanations of the correct answers are given. The explanations will help you understand how to think through these question types.

   If you have any questions about how to complete the exercises or score them, this is the time to get the answers.

Working Through Each Lesson.   Begin each lesson by looking at the photograph and reading the caption. Before you read, predict what you think the article will be about. Then read the article.

   Sometimes your teacher may decide to time your reading. Timing helps you keep track of and increase your reading speed. If you have been timed, enter your reading time in the box at the end of the lesson. Then use the Words-per-Minute Table to find your reading speed, and record your speed on the Reading Speed graph at the end of the unit.

   Next complete the Reading Comprehension and Critical Thinking exercises. The directions for each exercise will tell you how to mark your answers. When you have finished all four Reading Comprehension exercises, use the answer key provided by your teacher to check your work. Follow the directions after each exercise to find your score. Record your Reading Comprehension scores on the graph at the end of each unit. Then check your answers to the Author's Approach, Summarizing and Paraphrasing, and Critical Thinking exercises. Fill in the Critical Thinking chart at the end of each unit with your evaluation of your work and comments about your progress.

   At the end of each unit you will also complete a Compare and Contrast chart. The completed chart will help you see what the articles have in common, and it will give you an opportunity to explore your own ideas about the events in the articles.

SAMPLE LESSON

The Legend of Billy the Kid

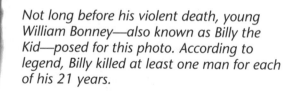

Not long before his violent death, young William Bonney—also known as Billy the Kid—posed for this photo. According to legend, Billy killed at least one man for each of his 21 years.

Legend says that Billy the Kid killed one man for each of the 21 years of his life. That may or may not be true. Tales about this young outlaw are often overblown. It is hard to find the truth. Billy might have killed "only" 19 or as many as 27 men before he was gunned down in 1881. The exact number is not important. What is important is the way Billy stands out in history. Hundreds of books have been written about him. Most picture him as a romantic symbol of the Old West. But in fact, he was a heartless killer.

2   Billy the Kid, also known as William Bonney, was born in New York City. When he was a young boy, his family moved to Silver City, New Mexico. Billy began his life of crime early. There was no school in his hometown of Silver City, New Mexico, so little Billy spent his time playing in the streets. He learned to gamble and to steal. He learned to fight with his fists. And he learned to use a gun.

3   The first man he killed was Frank Cahill. Apparently, Cahill called Billy a name. He was half joking. But Billy didn't think it was very funny. He hit Cahill. Then Cahill, a grown man, knocked 14-year-old Billy to the ground. That was a mistake. Flushed with anger, Billy drew his gun and shot Cahill.

4   Billy was put in jail, but he escaped a few nights later. He became a drifter. From time to time, he worked as a cowboy. He also made money playing cards. One night Billy accused a fellow gambler of cheating. The man just laughed at Billy, calling him a "billy goat." A moment later, the man was lying dead on the floor with a bullet hole between his eyes.

5   Billy's real killing spree began in 1878. He was 19 years old. By then, he had hooked up with a man named John Tunstall. Tunstall, it was later said, was the Kid's one true friend. In fact, Billy called Tunstall "the only man that ever treated me [fairly]." Unfortunately, Tunstall had many enemies. One day a group of 25 men hunted him down. They shot him in cold blood. Billy witnessed the killing but was too far away to stop it. According to legend, Billy swore an oath at Tunstall's grave. "I'll get every [man] who helped kill John if it's the last thing I do."

6   Billy the Kid kept his word. He tracked down and shot every person who had played a part in Tunstall's death. One of these men was Sheriff William Brady. When Billy shot Brady, he gave himself a death sentence. He had killed a lawman. Now other lawmen came after him. They vowed to settle the score. Sheriff Pat Garrett tracked Billy for two years. In 1881 Garrett trapped him. Billy was arrested and brought to trial. He was found guilty of killing Brady. Judge Warren Bristol ordered Billy to be hanged until "you are dead, dead, dead."

7   But again Billy the Kid escaped.

Fifteen days before he was supposed to be hanged, Billy somehow got his hands on a gun. He shot his guards. Then he took off into the New Mexico wilderness.

8   Sheriff Garrett formed a posse. He went after Billy again. For three months, he stalked him. At last, Garrett got a tip. He heard that Billy was staying at the Maxwell ranch near the town of Fort Sumner. Just past midnight on July 14, 1881, Garrett slipped into Maxwell's bedroom off the front porch. Billy, hearing noises, walked down the porch. He peeked into Maxwell's dark room.

9   "Who's that?" the Kid called out.

10   Garrett answered with two shots. The first bullet struck Billy just above the heart. The Kid died on the spot. Sheriff Garrett rushed out of the room, shouting, "I killed the Kid! I killed the Kid!"

A Finding the Main Idea

One statement below expresses the main idea of the article. One statement is too general, or too broad. The other statement explains only part of the article; it is too narrow. Label the statements using the following key:

M—Main Idea   **B—Too Broad**   **N—Too Narrow**

___N___ 1. When Billy killed Sheriff Brady, he attracted the attention of lawmen throughout the West. [This statement is true, but it is *too narrow*. It gives only one piece, or detail, from the article.]

___B___ 2. Gunfighters have become symbols of the Old West in the American mind. [This statement is *too broad*. The article is about a particular gunfighter, Billy the Kid.]

___M___ 3. Billy the Kid was responsible for many killings before the law finally caught up with him. [This is the *main idea*. It tells whom the article is about—Billy the Kid. It also tells you what he did.]

___15___ Score 15 points for a correct M answer.

___10___ Score 5 points for each correct B or N answer.

___25___ **Total Score:** Finding the Main Idea

B Recalling Facts

How well do you remember the facts in the article? Put an X in the box next to the answer that correctly completes each statement about the article.

1. One thing that Billy did *not* do as a boy was
   ☐ a. learn how to use a gun.
   ☐ b. learn how to gamble.
   ☒ c. go to school.

2. According to legend, the first man Billy killed
   ☒ a. had insulted Billy and knocked him down.
   ☐ b. owed Billy money and wouldn't repay it.
   ☐ c. drew his gun on Billy first.

3. It is said that the only true friend that Billy ever had was
   ☐ a. William Brady.
   ☐ b. Pat Garrett.
   ☒ c. John Tunstall.

4. When Billy was found guilty of killing the sheriff, he was sentenced to be
   ☐ a. shot by a firing squad.
   ☒ b. hanged.
   ☐ c. kept in prison for the rest of his life.

5. Billy was finally gunned down
   ☒ a. at the Maxwell ranch near Fort Sumner.
   ☐ b. in Silver City, New Mexico.
   ☐ c. as he escaped from prison.

Score 5 points for each correct answer.

___25___ **Total Score:** Recalling Facts

C Making Inferences

When you combine your own experience with information from a text to draw a conclusion that is not directly stated in that text, you are making an inference. Below are five statements that may or may not be inferences based on information in the article. Label the statements using the following key:

C—Correct Inference   F—Faulty Inference

__F__ 1. Most killers in the Old West were famous and popular. [This is a faulty inference. Just because one killer became famous does not mean that most did.]

__C__ 2. What Billy saw and learned on the streets of Silver City probably affected his actions as an adult. [This is a correct inference. You are told that Billy learned violent and illegal skills in the streets.]

__C__ 3. When Billy made up his mind to do something, he did it. [This is a correct inference. Billy kept his vow to kill those who had killed his friend.]

__C__ 4. Billy had a quick temper and often acted right away when he got angry. [This is a correct inference. The article states that Billy shot his victims just after they offended him.]

__F__ 5. When Sheriff Pat Garrett ran into problems, he usually gave up easily. [This is a faulty inference. Sheriff Garrett tracked Billy for years before finally catching up to him.]

Score 5 points for each correct answer.

__25__ **Total Score:** Making Inferences

D Using Words Precisely

Each numbered sentence below contains an underlined word or phrase from the article. Following the sentence are three definitions. One definition is closest to the meaning of the underlined word. One definition is opposite or nearly opposite. Label those two definitions using the following key; do not label the remaining definition.

C—Closest   O—Opposite or Nearly Opposite

1. Tales about this young outlaw are often <u>overblown</u>.

__O__ a. understated

__C__ b. overdone

_____ c. exciting

2. Most picture him as a <u>romantic</u> symbol of the Old West.

__C__ a. not based on fact

__O__ b. realistic

_____ c. brave

3. He became a <u>drifter</u>.

__O__ a. person who likes to stay in one place

_____ b. person who shoots well

__C__ c. person who travels aimlessly

4. For three months, he <u>stalked</u> Billy.

_____ a. knew

__O__ b. avoided

__C__ c. followed

5. Billy <u>witnessed</u> the killing but was too far away to stop it.

   _C_   a. saw

  _____ b. was sorry about

   _O_   c. missed

   _15_   Score 3 points for each correct C answer.

   _10_   Score 2 points for each correct O answer.

   _25_   **Total Score:** Using Words Precisely

Enter the four total scores in the spaces below, and add them together to find your Reading Comprehension Score. Then record your score on the graph on page 57.

Score	Question Type	Sample Lesson
_____	Finding the Main Idea	
_____	Recalling Facts	
_____	Making Inferences	
_____	Using Words Precisely	
_____	**Reading Comprehension Score**	

Author's Approach

Put an X in the box next to the correct answer.

1. What do the authors mean by the statement "They shot him in cold blood"?

☐ a. They felt sad and sorry that they had to kill him.

☒ b. They killed him cruelly, without any emotion.

☐ c. They were feeling chilly, but they killed him anyway.

2. Judging by statements from the article "The Legend of Billy the Kid" you can conclude that the authors want the reader to think that

☐ a. Billy the Kid was a hero of the Old West.

☒ b. Billy the Kid was a cruel, heartless killer.

☐ c. although Billy committed a few crimes, he was basically a good person.

3. What do the authors imply by saying "Judge Warren Bristol ordered Billy to be hanged 'until you are dead, dead, dead'"?

☒ a. Judge Warren was angry and disgusted with Billy and was anxious to execute him.

☐ b. Judge Warren felt sorry that the young man's life had to end.

☐ c. Judge Warren often repeated his words three times.

4. The authors tell this story mainly by

☐ a. comparing different topics.

☐ b. using their imagination and creativity.

☒ c. describing events in the order they happened.

   _4_   Number of correct answers

Record your personal assessment of your work on the Critical Thinking Chart on page 58.

Summarizing and Paraphrasing

Follow the directions provided for question 1. Put an X in the box next to the correct answer for question 2.

1. Complete the following one-sentence summary of the article using the lettered phrases from the phrase bank below. Write the letters on the lines.

Phrase Bank

a. Billy's three-year killing spree

b. Billy's early life

c. Billy's death

The article "The Legend of Billy the Kid" begins with ___b___, goes on to describe ___a___, and ends with ___c___.

2. Read the statement about the article below. Then read the paraphrase of that statement. Choose the reason that best tells why the paraphrase does not say the same thing as the statement.

Statement: One legend says that Billy swore an oath to kill everyone who helped kill his friend John Tunstall, and he kept his word.

Paraphrase: Legend tells us that after John Tunstall's killing, Billy vowed that he would kill everyone who played a part in that crime.

☐ a. Paraphrase says too much.

☒ b. Paraphrase doesn't say enough. [This statement leaves out the detail that Billy actually fulfilled his vow.]

☐ c. Paraphrase doesn't agree with the statement.

___2___ Number of correct answers

Record your personal assessment of your work on the Critical Thinking Chart on page 58.

Critical Thinking

Follow the directions provided for questions 1, 2, and 3. Put an X in the box next to the correct answer for the other questions.

1. For each statement below, write O if it expresses an opinion or write F if it expresses a fact.

___F___ a. Billy the Kid grew up in Silver City, New Mexico.

___O___ b. Billy the Kid was the meanest outlaw in the Old West.

___F___ c. Billy the Kid was shot and killed by Sheriff Pat Garrett.

2. Choose from the letters below to correctly complete the following statement. Write the letters on the lines.

On the positive side, ___c___, but on the negative side ___b___.

a. Billy the Kid's best friend was John Tunstall

b. Billy the Kid may have killed a man for each year of his short life

c. Sheriff Pat Garrett was successful in finally stopping Billy the Kid's killing spree

3. Reread paragraph 4. Then choose from the letters below to correctly complete the following statement. Write the letters on the lines.

   According to paragraph 4, ___a___ because ___c___ .

   a. Billy shot a gambler who he thought was cheating at cards

   b. Billy escaped from jail

   c. a gambler called Billy a "billy goat"

4. How is "The Legend of Billy the Kid" related to the theme of *Crime and Punishment*?

   ☐ a. Billy the Kid stands out in history as a romantic hero, possibly because he was so young when he died.

   ☐ b. Billy the Kid was arrested several times but always managed to escape from jail.

   ☒ c. Billy the Kid killed many people and was finally shot and killed for his crimes.

5. What did you have to do to answer question 3?

   ☒ a. find a cause (why something happened)

   ☐ b. find an opinion (what someone thinks about something)

   ☐ c. find a comparison (how things are the same)

   ___5___ Number of correct answers

   Record your personal assessment of your work on the Critical Thinking Chart on page 58.

Personal Response

What new question do you have about this topic?

___[Do you want to know more about Billy the Kid, Sheriff Pat Garrett,___

___or the Old West? On the lines, write one new question that occurred to___

___you while you read the article or after you finished reading it.]___

Self-Assessment

Before reading this article, I already knew _____

___[Write something you already knew about Billy the Kid or the Old West before___

___reading this article.]___

Self-Assessment

To get the most out of the *Wild Side* series, you need to take charge of your own progress in improving your reading comprehension and critical thinking skills. Here are some of the features that help you work on those essential skills.

Reading Comprehension Exercises.   Complete these exercises immediately after reading each article. They help you recall what you have read, understand the stated and implied main ideas, and add words to your working vocabulary.

Critical Thinking Skills Exercises.   These exercises help you focus on the author's approach and purpose, recognize and generate summaries and paraphrases, and identify relationships between ideas.

Personal Response and Self-Assessment.   Questions in this category help you relate the articles to your personal experience and give you the opportunity to evaluate your understanding of the information in that lesson.

Compare and Contrast Charts.   At the end of each unit you will complete a Compare and Contrast chart. The completed chart helps you see what the articles have in common and gives you an opportunity to explore your own ideas about the topics discussed in the articles.

The Graphs.   The graphs and charts at the end of each unit enable you to keep track of your progress. Check your graphs regularly with your teacher. Decide whether your progress is satisfactory or whether you need additional work on some skills. What types of exercises are you having difficulty with? Talk with your teacher about ways to work on the skills in which you need the most practice.

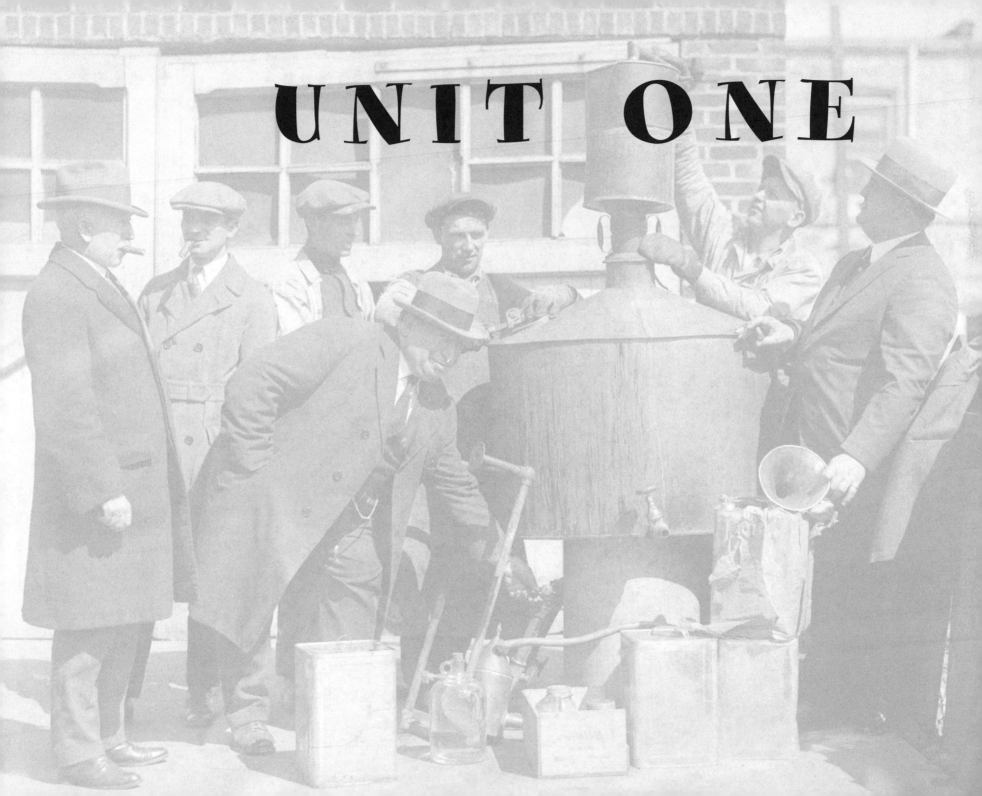

UNIT ONE

Bonnie and Clyde

He was the "Texas Rattlesnake." She was "Suicide Sal." Together they drove through Texas, robbing and killing at every turn. They never got rich. In fact, they never managed to steal more than $1,500 at any one time. But they left a trail of blood across the land. It was this willingness to kill that made Bonnie and Clyde famous. From April 1932 until May 1934, they shot and killed a dozen people.

2   Bonnie Parker met Clyde Barrow in 1930. She was a 19-year-old waitress

Early in their careers in crime, Bonnie Parker and Clyde Barrow took time out for some horseplay. In this photo taken by a gang member, Bonnie pretends to rob Clyde at gunpoint. Later, they left the photo behind while escaping a raid.

who was bored with life. She wanted excitement and danger. That was exactly what 21-year-old Clyde seemed to offer. Clyde liked to gamble. He also liked to steal cars. When he needed money, he robbed stores or gas stations. Bonnie decided to hook up with him and have some "fun."

3 Unfortunately for Bonnie, Clyde wasn't a very good thief. At one break-in, he forgot to wear gloves. He left fingerprints all over the place. Soon after Bonnie met him, he was caught and sent to jail.

4 Bonnie could have walked away from Clyde right then. But she didn't. She was in love with him. So she visited him in jail, slipping him a gun that she had taped to her leg. That night, Clyde broke out of jail. He was quickly recaptured, however, and sent to Eastman, one of the toughest prisons in the country. Clyde served two years there. When he got out, he was angry and bitter. He vowed never to spend another day in prison. "I'll die first," he declared.

5 Clyde meant what he said. With Bonnie at his side, he began robbing again. But now he was tougher. In fact, he was ruthless. He carried guns wherever he went. And he was ready to use them. On April 28, 1932, Clyde robbed a jewelry store in Hillsboro, Texas. He still wasn't a very smooth criminal, however, and during the robbery he panicked. He shot the 65-year-old owner through the heart.

6 Now Clyde was a murderer as well as a thief. Still, Bonnie remained loyal to him. In fact, she became as cold and hard as he was. To her, killing became a kind of joke. She had Clyde take pictures of her holding a machine gun. In one photo, she pretended to be robbing Clyde. In another, she and Clyde were both holding pistols and grinning wildly.

7 Like Clyde, Bonnie figured she would die young. She fully expected to be shot full of police bullets someday. That attitude earned her the nickname Suicide Sal. Bonnie actually wrote a poem by that title. The poem told the story of a woman who fell in love with a "professional killer." One part read:

I couldn't help loving him madly;
For him even now I would die.

8 Bonnie also wrote a poem called "The Story of Bonnie and Clyde." It included these lines:

They don't think they're too tough or desperate,
They know that the law always wins;
They've been shot at before,
But they do not ignore
That death is the wages of sin.

9 By the spring of 1933, Bonnie and Clyde had murdered seven people. They killed an old shopkeeper for $28. Clyde killed a sheriff and a deputy who spoke to him at a barn dance. Clyde shot one man on Christmas Day just so he could take a ride in the man's car.

10 That June, Bonnie and Clyde were traveling down a country road. Clyde was driving. He was usually an excellent driver. But on this day, he failed to see that a bridge was closed for repairs. He tried to stop at the last minute, but it was too late. The car flew over a steep bank, crashed, and exploded in a ball of fire. Clyde was thrown clear of the wreck. Bonnie, however, was trapped in the flames.

By the time Clyde pulled her out, her whole body was badly burned.

11   Clyde took her to a nearby farmhouse. There a farmer's wife bandaged Bonnie as best she could. But Bonnie was in terrible pain. For a while, it looked as though she might die. Clyde nursed Bonnie all summer. He also continued to rob and kill. He rounded up some other thugs to help him. One was his brother Buck.

12   That July, Buck was killed in a shoot-out with police. It happened at a park where the outlaws were camping. Clyde and Bonnie were there, too, but they managed to escape. Although Clyde was hit with four bullets, he did not fall. He helped Bonnie swim across a river. Then he stole a car and whisked her up into the hills.

13   Bonnie and Clyde spent the next few weeks in misery. Both of them needed medical attention. But they didn't dare go to a hospital. So, as Bonnie put it, "we lived in little ravines, secluded woods, down side roads for days that stretched into weeks. We were . . . so sick that time went by without our knowing it. We lost track of the days."

14   By September, Clyde was feeling better. He took Bonnie to visit her mother, Emma Parker. Mrs. Parker was horrified by her daughter's appearance. She said, "Bonnie was . . . unable to walk without help. She was miserably thin and looked much older. Her leg was drawn up under her. Her body was covered in scars."

15   Time was clearly running out for Bonnie and Clyde. Winter came. Still, the couple often had to sleep out in the open or in their unheated car. They moved from place to place, sticking to backwoods and small towns. By now, though, they weren't safe anywhere. A lawman named Frank Hamer was closing in on them.

16   In May of 1934, Hamer and his men set up an ambush near Gibland, Louisiana. On May 24, Bonnie and Clyde approached in a stolen car. Hamer's men shouted at them to halt. Said one officer, "We wished to give them a chance."

17   "But," added Hamer, "they both reached for their guns."

18   Before Bonnie or Clyde could get off a shot, officers blasted them with a total of 187 bullets.

19   Clyde slumped in his seat, dead. Bonnie, too, died instantly. The car crashed into a hillside. When Hamer and his men got to it, they found a machine gun lying in Bonnie's lap. Clyde's hand still rested on a sawed-off shotgun.

20   In the end, then, Bonnie Parker had been right. She had predicted this day would come. Her poem called "The Story of Bonnie and Clyde" concluded with these words:

> Some day they'll go down
>   together;
> And they'll bury them side by side;
> To a few it'll be grief—
> To the law a relief—
> But it's death for Bonnie and Clyde.

If you have been timed while reading this article, enter your reading time below. Then turn to the Words-per-Minute Table on page 55 and look up your reading speed (words per minute). Enter your reading speed on the graph on page 56.

Reading Time: Lesson 1

_____ : _____
Minutes   Seconds

A | Finding the Main Idea

One statement below expresses the main idea of the article. One statement is too general, or too broad. The other statement explains only part of the article; it is too narrow. Label the statements using the following key:

M—Main Idea   **B—Too Broad**   **N—Too Narrow**

_____ 1. Bonnie Parker and Clyde Barrrow were two of the most famous criminals in the United States during the 1930s.

_____ 2. The murderers Bonnie Parker and Clyde Barrow were killed in a shower of bullets during an ambush by lawmen led by agent Frank Hamer.

_____ 3. Although they were poor thieves, Bonnie Parker and Clyde Barrow became famous for their murdering ways and their loyalty to each other.

_____ Score 15 points for a correct M answer.

_____ Score 5 points for each correct B or N answer.

_____ **Total Score:** Finding the Main Idea

B | Recalling Facts

How well do you remember the facts in the article? Put an X in the box next to the answer that correctly completes each statement about the article.

1. Bonnie Parker first met Clyde Barrow
□ a. when he was 19 years old.
□ b. when she was 19 years old.
□ c. in 1919.

2. Clyde committed his first murder
□ a. during a jewelry store robbery.
□ b. in the course of a car theft.
□ c. when he broke out of jail with the gun Bonnie had brought him.

3. Bonnie wrote about her life as a criminal in
□ a. an autobiography published after her death.
□ b. letters to the editors of newspapers.
□ c. poems about herself and Clyde.

4. Bonnie was seriously injured
□ a. in a shoot-out at her mother's home.
□ b. in a fire caused by a car accident.
□ c. when she was playing with guns.

5. Before Hamer and his men opened fire on Bonnie and Clyde, the
□ a. lawmen had a long conversation with them in an effort to get them to surrender.
□ b. outlaws tried to run down the officers.
□ c. lawmen saw them reach for their guns.

Score 5 points for each correct answer.

_____ **Total Score:** Recalling Facts

C Making Inferences

When you combine your own experience with information from a text to draw a conclusion that is not directly stated in that text, you are making an inference. Below are five statements that may or may not be inferences based on information in the article. Label the statements using the following key:

C—Correct Inference   **F—Faulty Inference**

_____ 1. If Bonnie had known that Clyde would become a killer, she would never have fallen in love with him.

_____ 2. Clyde Barrow became a criminal to impress Bonnie Parker.

_____ 3. Bonnie wrote poetry because she figured her readers would become sympathetic and would forgive her and Clyde for the crimes they committed.

_____ 4. Bonnie put her own mother in danger by coming to visit her.

_____ 5. If Frank Hamer's men had been more patient, Bonnie and Clyde probably would have surrendered peacefully.

Score 5 points for each correct answer.

_____ **Total Score:** Making Inferences

D Using Words Precisely

Each numbered sentence below contains an underlined word or phrase from the article. Following the sentence are three definitions. One definition is closest to the meaning of the underlined word. One definition is opposite or nearly opposite. Label those two definitions using the following key; do not label the remaining definition.

C—Closest   **O—Opposite or Nearly Opposite**

1. In fact, he was <u>ruthless</u>.

_____ a. without mercy

_____ b. helpless

_____ c. kind

2. They don't think they're too tough or <u>desperate</u>.

_____ a. hopeful

_____ b. frantic; reckless

_____ c. considerate

3. Then he stole a car and <u>whisked</u> her up into the hills.

_____ a. slowly carried

_____ b. whistled

_____ c. quickly moved

4. So, as Bonnie put it, "we lived in little ravines, <u>secluded</u> woods, down side roads for days that stretched into weeks."

_____ a. open

_____ b. hidden; private

_____ c. shady

5. Her poem called "The Story of Bonnie and Clyde" <u>concluded</u> with these words: ". . . it's death for Bonnie and Clyde."

_____ a. began

_____ b. sang

_____ c. ended

_____ Score 3 points for each correct C answer.

_____ Score 2 points for each correct O answer.

_____ **Total Score:** Using Words Precisely

Enter the four total scores in the spaces below, and add them together to find your Reading Comprehension Score. Then record your score on the graph on page 57.

Score	Question Type	Lesson 1
_____	Finding the Main Idea	
_____	Recalling Facts	
_____	Making Inferences	
_____	Using Words Precisely	
_____	**Reading Comprehension Score**	

Author's Approach

1. The main purpose of the first paragraph is to

☐ a. summarize Bonnie and Clyde's careers in crime.

☐ b. explain why Bonnie and Clyde robbed and killed.

☐ c. persuade the reader to like Bonnie and Clyde.

2. Which of the following statements from the article best describes Bonnie at the time she met Clyde?

☐ a. She was miserably thin and looked much older.

☐ b. She was a 19-year-old waitress who was bored with life.

☐ c. She fully expected to be shot full of police bullets someday.

3. Judging by statements from the article "Bonnie and Clyde," you can conclude that the authors want the reader to think that

☐ a. a life of crime is glamorous.

☐ b. Bonnie and Clyde's crimes ruined their lives.

☐ c. Bonnie and Clyde's crimes were not very serious.

4. In this article, "Time was clearly running out for Bonnie and Clyde" means

☐ a. Bonnie and Clyde were tired of crime and were ready to start living a normal life.

☐ b. it was time for Bonnie and Clyde to commit another robbery.

☐ c. Bonnie and Clyde would probably not be able to continue their lives of crime for much longer.

_____ Number of correct answers

Record your personal assessment of your work on the Critical Thinking Chart on page 58.

Summarizing and Paraphrasing

Follow the directions provided for question 1. Put an X in the box next to the correct answer for the other questions.

1. Complete the following one-sentence summary of the article using the lettered phrases from the phrase bank below. Write the letters on the lines.

> **Phrase Bank**
> a. the difficulties Bonnie and Clyde faced during their life of crime
> b. the deaths of Bonnie and Clyde
> c. a description of Bonnie and Clyde's early crimes

The article "Bonnie and Clyde" begins with _____, goes on

to explain _____, and ends with _____.

2. Below are summaries of the article. Choose the summary that says all the most important things about the article but in the fewest words.

☐ a. In a two-year crime spree from 1932 to 1934, Bonnie Parker and Clyde Barrow robbed and killed many times. They were finally ambushed by police and killed in a rain of bullets.

☐ b. Bonnie Parker met Clyde Barrow in 1930 and joined him on his crime spree. Bonnie wrote poetry about their lives.

☐ c. Clyde Barrow was a small-time robber when he met 19-year-old Bonnie Parker in 1930. After he broke out of jail, with Bonnie's help, he robbed a jewelry store in Texas and killed its owner. From then on, he was on the run, along with Bonnie.

3. Choose the best one-sentence paraphrase for the following sentence from the article: "By the time Clyde pulled [Bonnie] out, her whole body was badly burned."

☐ a. Clyde's body was badly burned by the time Clyde pulled Bonnie from the fire.

☐ b. In pulling Bonnie from the fire, Clyde burned himself badly.

☐ c. Before Clyde could pull Bonnie out of the fire, she had been badly burned.

_____ Number of correct answers

Record your personal assessment of your work on the Critical Thinking Chart on page 58.

Critical Thinking

Follow the directions provided for questions 1, 3, and 5. Put an X in the box next to the correct answer for the other questions.

1. For each statement below, write *O* if it expresses an opinion or write *F* if it expresses a fact.

_____ a. Bonnie and Clyde were not very intelligent.

_____ b. The police could have taken Bonnie and Clyde alive if they had wanted to.

_____ c. Clyde's brother, Buck, was killed in a shoot-out with police.

2. From the article, you can predict that if Hamer had waited a few minutes more for Bonnie and Clyde to surrender,

☐ a. the criminals would have surrendered to him without a fight.

☐ b. the criminals would have shot and maybe killed some of his men.

☐ c. most citizens would have approved of his actions because they would have been more honorable.

3. Choose from the letters below to correctly complete the following statement. Write the letters on the lines.

On the positive side, _____, but on the negative side,

_____.

a. loving Clyde caused Bonnie to become a criminal herself

b. Bonnie had been a waitress before she met Clyde

c. Bonnie really loved Clyde

4. What was the cause of the car accident in which Bonnie was badly burned?

☐ a. The police shot Clyde as he was driving, making him run off the road.

☐ b. Clyde couldn't stop at a bridge that was closed for repairs.

☐ c. The owner of the car shot Clyde, who then ran off the road.

5. In which paragraph did you find your information or details to answer question 4? _____

_____ Number of correct answers

Record your personal assessment of your work on the Critical Thinking Chart on page 58.

Personal Response

A question I would like answered by Bonnie Parker is _____

_____

_____

_____

Self-Assessment

I was confused about question _____ in the _____ section

because _____

_____

_____

_____

Izzy and Moe

They had funny names: Izzy and Moe. And these two guys really *were* funny! People around the country laughed when they read about Izzy and Moe's latest tricks. It seemed that each new stunt was funnier than the last one. But Izzy and Moe were not a circus act or a comedy team. They were cops.

2   In 1919 a new law was passed. The law made it illegal to manufacture, sell, or transport liquor. This law was canceled in 1933. But for 14 years, people were not allowed to use liquor. That meant beer and wine were out.

During Prohibition, when making and selling liquor became illegal, bootleggers feared government agents. Izzy Einstein and Moe Smith, the stout gentlemen on either side of this illegal still, were two of the flashiest agents.

3   So were gin, whiskey, and all other drinks containing alcohol. This time period was called *Prohibition*. That's because people were prohibited from having alcohol.

4   Many people ignored the new law. They thought it was wrong. They said the government had no right to deny them a bottle of beer or a glass of wine. Some people smuggled liquor into the country. These people were called *bootleggers*. Other people made their own booze—liquor—at home. "Bathtub gin" became a favorite. And all over America, people slipped into illegal bars called *speakeasies*. Customers had to "speak easy" so they would not attract the attention of the police.

5   The police, meanwhile, were trying to enforce the law. That's where Izzy and Moe came in. Izzy Einstein and Moe Smith were government agents. Their job was to find people serving or drinking liquor and to arrest them. To do this, Izzy and Moe dressed in disguises. Some of their costumes were quite outrageous. They used smiles and laughs in order to trap bar owners. They were friendly with everyone— until it was time to make an arrest!

6   One night Izzy and Moe dressed up as football players. They knocked on a speakeasy door in New York City. "We won the game!" they shouted. "Let us in. We want to celebrate with a pint [of beer]."

7   The bar owner laughed and let them in. He praised them for their victory. Then he got them each a beer. But his smile quickly faded when Izzy and Moe flashed their badges. The two agents arrested the man for serving them liquor.

8   Then there was the time Izzy and Moe wore dresses. Pretending to be ladies who had just come from the theater, they entered a restaurant. The two "ladies" ordered a small meal. All the time, their eyes scanned the restaurant. Izzy and Moe were looking for signs that the owner was selling liquor. They found plenty of clues. The next day, police raided the place. They found more than $10,000 worth of smuggled liquor.

9   Once Izzy and Moe dressed up as car mechanics. They found 200 cases of whiskey in a garage. One time they dressed as gravediggers and raided a bar near a graveyard. Once they put

on long black coats and carried violin cases. Their target? A bar that served only musicians. At times they also posed as horse traders, farmers, and rabbis.

10   Izzy and Moe's fame spread rapidly. "Be careful," bar owners would warn each other. "Izzy and Moe are in the neighborhood." Most owners came to hate these two agents.

11   Once Izzy walked into a bar alone. He looked up and saw his own photograph hanging over the bar. The owner had put black cloth around it to show that he wished Izzy were dead. Izzy went ahead and ordered a drink. It must not have been a very good photo of him, because the bartender didn't recognize him. Still, the man wouldn't pour Izzy a drink.

12   "I don't know you," the bartender said. (In those days, bartenders often refused to serve people they didn't know. They were worried about being caught by agents like Izzy and Moe.)

13   "Sure you know me," Izzy said. "I'm Izzy Epstein, the famous agent."

14   "You don't even have the name right," the bartender said with a laugh. "That guy's name is Einstein."

15   Izzy insisted that the name was Epstein. At last, he offered to bet the bartender a drink about it. The bartender agreed. He poured out two drinks. To settle the bet, Izzy pulled out his badge. He arrested the bartender on the spot.

16   Izzy and Moe came to the end of the line in 1925. They were dismissed from their jobs. The reason isn't clear. At the time, their bosses said Izzy and Moe had become too famous. Too many people recognized them. That meant they were no longer as useful as they had once been.

17   That might not have been the real reason. Some other agents resented Izzy and Moe's success. Still other agents feared their honesty. After all, some agents were crooks. They were paid by bootleggers to look the other way. Perhaps these crooked agents thought Izzy and Moe would find out about their deals. These agents might

have arranged to get Izzy and Moe fired.

18   In any case, Izzy and Moe had built up quite a record. In four years, they arrested more than 4,000 people. They also destroyed more than five million bottles of liquor!

If you have been timed while reading this article, enter your reading time below. Then turn to the Words-per-Minute Table on page 55 and look up your reading speed (words per minute). Enter your reading speed on the graph on page 56.

Reading Time: Lesson 2

_____ : _____
Minutes   Seconds

A Finding the Main Idea

One statement below expresses the main idea of the article. One statement is too general, or too broad. The other statement explains only part of the article; it is too narrow. Label the statements using the following key:

M—Main Idea   B—Too Broad   N—Too Narrow

_____ 1. Izzy Einstein and Moe Smith dressed as women, rabbis, and farmers to trick bar owners.

_____ 2. During Prohibition, Izzy Einstein and Moe Smith became famous across the United States.

_____ 3. During Prohibition, Izzy Einstein and Moe Smith were colorful and effective government agents.

_____ Score 15 points for a correct M answer.

_____ Score 5 points for each correct B or N answer.

_____ **Total Score:** Finding the Main Idea

B Recalling Facts

How well do you remember the facts in the article? Put an X in the box next to the answer that correctly completes each statement about the article.

1. During Prohibition, people were not allowed to
   ☐ a. vote against liquor.
   ☐ b. go to circus acts.
   ☐ c. make, sell, or transport liquor.

2. Bootleggers were people who
   ☐ a. smuggled liquor into the country.
   ☐ b. made their own booze at home.
   ☐ c. were customers at speakeasies.

3. Izzy and Moe dressed up in disguises in order to
   ☐ a. get a great deal of publicity.
   ☐ b. win prizes at contests at the bars.
   ☐ c. trick people at bars and speakeasies.

4. Izzy's picture was hanging in one bar because
   ☐ a. he was so well liked by the bar owner.
   ☐ b. the bar owner wished he were dead.
   ☐ c. he was quite a handsome man.

5. When Izzy and Moe lost their jobs with the government, their bosses said the reason was that they were too
   ☐ a. honest.
   ☐ b. famous.
   ☐ c. old.

Score 5 points for each correct answer.

_____ **Total Score:** Recalling Facts

C Making Inferences

When you combine your own experience with information from a text to draw a conclusion that is not directly stated in that text, you are making an inference. Below are five statements that may or may not be inferences based on information in the article. Label the statements using the following key:

C—Correct Inference   **F—Faulty Inference**

_____ 1. In general, U.S. citizens finally decided that a law against using liquor had little or no benefit.

_____ 2. The liquor used in speakeasies was almost always of poor quality.

_____ 3. Most of the people who broke the liquor laws during Prohibition had long criminal records.

_____ 4. During Prohibition, people who wanted a drink did not have a hard time finding bars that would serve them.

_____ 5. If Izzy and Moe had stayed on the job, they might have been in danger from their fellow agents.

Score 5 points for each correct answer.

_____ **Total Score:** Making Inferences

D Using Words Precisely

Each numbered sentence below contains an underlined word or phrase from the article. Following the sentence are three definitions. One definition is closest to the meaning of the underlined word. One definition is opposite or nearly opposite. Label those two definitions using the following key; do not label the remaining definition.

C—Closest   **O—Opposite or Nearly Opposite**

1. That's because people were <u>prohibited from</u> having alcohol.

_____ a. encouraged in

_____ b. prevented from

_____ c. made ill by

2. The police, meanwhile, were trying to <u>enforce</u> the law.

_____ a. demand obedience to

_____ b. get rid of; ignore

_____ c. think about

3. Some of their costumes were quite <u>outrageous</u>.

_____ a. expensive

_____ b. strange

_____ c. boring; not easily noticed

4. All the time, their eyes <u>scanned</u> the restaurant.

_____ a. shut out

_____ b. blinked inside

_____ c. checked over

5. They were <u>dismissed from</u> their jobs.

_____ a. fired from

_____ b. given ratings at

_____ c. employed at

_____ Score 3 points for each correct C answer.

_____ Score 2 points for each correct O answer.

_____ **Total Score:** Using Words Precisely

Enter the four total scores in the spaces below, and add them together to find your Reading Comprehension Score. Then record your score on the graph on page 57.

Score	Question Type	Lesson 2
_____	Finding the Main Idea	
_____	Recalling Facts	
_____	Making Inferences	
_____	Using Words Precisely	
_____	**Reading Comprehension Score**	

Author's Approach

Put an X in the box next to the correct answer.

1. What is the authors' purpose in writing "Izzy and Moe"?

☐ a. to encourage the reader to learn more about bootleggers

☐ b. to inform the reader about the work of two federal agents during Prohibition

☐ c. to express an opinion about whether people should drink liquor

2. Which of the following statements from the article best describes Izzy and Moe?

☐ a. Izzy Einstein and Moe Smith were government agents.

☐ b. Izzy and Moe were not a circus act or a comedy team.

☐ c. Izzy and Moe's fame spread rapidly.

3. From the statements below, choose those that you believe the authors would agree with.

☐ a. Izzy and Moe enjoyed their job most of the time.

☐ b. Izzy and Moe did their job well.

☐ c. Izzy and Moe didn't take their job seriously enough.

4. Choose the statement below that best describes the authors' position in paragraph 17.

☐ a. Izzy and Moe worked as agents for four years.

☐ b. Liquor is evil and should be destroyed.

☐ c. Izzy and Moe were amazingly effective agents.

_____ Number of correct answers

Record your personal assessment of your work on the Critical Thinking Chart on page 58.

Summarizing and Paraphrasing

Follow the directions provided for question 1. Put an X in the box next to the correct answer for the other questions.

1. Look for the important ideas and events in paragraphs 5 and 6. Summarize those paragraphs in one or two sentences.

_____

_____

_____

_____

2. Below are summaries of the article. Choose the summary that says all the most important things about the article but in the fewest words.

☐ a. Izzy and Moe were probably the most famous federal agents during Prohibition even though they worked only four years. They may have been dismissed because crooked agents were afraid of them.

☐ b. Usually, when Izzy Einstein and Moe Smith walked into a speakeasy, no one recognized them because they were dressed in disguises. With their friendly way of talking, no one knew that they were federal agents until they showed their badges.

☐ c. Izzy and Moe were two famous federal agents who used smiles and costumes to catch bootleggers serving alcohol during Prohibition. Before they were dismissed from their jobs, they made many arrests and destroyed many bottles of liquor.

3. Choose the sentence that correctly restates the following sentence from the article: "[Crooked agents] were paid by bootleggers to look the other way."

☐ a. Crooked agents were paid by bootleggers for looking exactly like agents were expected to look.

☐ b. Crooked agents paid bootleggers not to look at them.

☐ c. Bootleggers paid crooked agents to ignore the fact that they were serving liquor.

> _____ Number of correct answers
>
> Record your personal assessment of your work on the Critical Thinking Chart on page 58.

Critical Thinking

Put an X in the box next to the correct answer for questions 1, 2, 4, and 5. Follow the directions provided for question 3.

1. Which of the following statements from the article is an opinion rather than a fact?

☐ a. Perhaps these crooked agents thought Izzy and Moe would find out about their deals.

☐ b. The law made it illegal to manufacture, sell, or transport liquor.

☐ c. They found 200 cases of whiskey in a garage.

2. Considering bar owners' actions as described in this article, you can predict that each time Izzy and Moe would fool them, the bar owners would feel

☐ a. embarrassed and angry.

☐ b. sorry for Izzy and Moe.

☐ c. pleased and grateful.

3. Choose from the letters below to correctly complete the following statement. Write the letters on the lines.

According to the article, _____ caused bar owners to _____, and the effect was _____.

a. trust Izzy and Moe and serve them drinks

b. Izzy and Moe's disguises and friendly manner

c. the bar owners were arrested

4. If you were a police detective today, how could you use Izzy and Moe's methods to catch criminals?

☐ a. go to places where alcohol is served

☐ b. destroy the criminals' liquor

☐ c. gain the criminals' trust and then catch them committing a crime

5. What did you have to do to answer question 3?

☐ a. find a cause (why something happened)

☐ b. draw a conclusion (a sensible statement based on the text and your experience)

☐ c. find a description (how something looks)

_____ Number of correct answers

Record your personal assessment of your work on the Critical Thinking Chart on page 58.

Personal Response

If I were the author, I would add _____

_____

because_____

_____

_____

Self-Assessment

From reading this article, I have learned _____

_____

_____

_____

Kidnapped!

At first no one believed that John Paul Getty III, grandson of the richest man in the world, had been kidnapped. Then a grisly envelope arrived, and everything changed.

Italian police thought it was a hoax. They did not believe 16-year-old John Paul Getty III had been kidnapped. A ransom note had been sent to Getty's mother. But it did not convince them. The note read:

Dear Mother:

I have fallen into the hands of kidnappers. Don't let me be killed! Make sure that the police do not interfere. You must absolutely not take this as a joke.

2   The note then demanded $17 million for the boy's safe return.

3   Police had reasons to be dubious. Getty's grandfather was the richest man in the world. Yet young Paul was always running out of money. Neither his father nor his grandfather would give him the cash he wanted. Paul himself had never earned any money on his own. He had dropped out of high school. He had no job. His idea of a tough day was going to a big party. Just before he disappeared, he joked about his lack of funds. He knew of a way to solve his money problems, he told friends with a laugh. All he had to do was stage his own "perfect kidnapping."

4   That explains why police were not too alarmed when he disappeared on July 10, 1973. They did investigate, of course. They looked around. They asked a few questions. But privately they thought the whole thing had been set up by Paul. They waited to see what Grandfather Getty would do. Would he come up with money to "save" his missing grandson?

5   Old Mr. Getty answered that question right away. "I'm against paying any money," he snapped. "It only encourages kidnappers." These words upset Gail Getty, mother of the missing boy. She believed her son was in real danger. "At first I thought it might be a stupid joke," she told one person. "But then I understood it was serious." With old Mr. Getty refusing to help, Gail feared her son might soon be killed. She announced that she would try to raise the ransom money herself.

6   But Gail did not have that kind of cash. She was divorced from John Paul Getty, Jr. So she couldn't get her hands on the Getty fortune. Meanwhile, her ex-husband agreed with his father. No money would be paid out.

7   The weeks dragged by. Then, in November, something happened that changed everything. An envelope was sent to an Italian newspaper. When employees opened it, they found a gruesome sight. The envelope contained a note, a lock of Paul's red hair, and a human ear.

8   "This is Paul's first ear," read the note. "If within 10 days the family still believes that this is a joke mounted by him, then the other ear will arrive. In other words, he will arrive in little bits."

9   Medical experts checked out the ear. It was Paul's. The boy's father and grandfather were shocked. They now realized that the kidnapping was real. Fearing for Paul's life, they agreed to bargain with the kidnappers. They

would not pay $17 million, they said. But they would hand over $2.8 million.

10 The kidnappers took that deal. They told the Getty family to put the money in three plastic bags. These bags were to be left along the side of a road in southern Italy. The Gettys did this. But first they had the police photograph each bill. That way the money could be traced. After the ransom money was delivered, the Gettys sat back to wait. They hoped and prayed that Paul would be returned to them.

11 On December 14, Gail Getty got a late-night phone call from the kidnappers. They had received the money, they said. They were about to release her son. Early the next morning, a truck driver named Antonio Tedesco saw a young man standing by the side of the road. It was raining hard. Yet the young man was not wearing a raincoat. He was standing in wet clothes, waving his arms wildly. Tedesco slowed down. He saw that the young man was crying. As Tedesco

pulled to a stop, the youth staggered over to the truck.

12 "I am Paul Getty," he said.

13 And so, five months after being kidnapped, John Paul Getty III was free. It turned out that he had suffered greatly during his five months as a hostage. The kidnappers had kept him blindfolded most of the time. They had forced him to march from one mountain hideout to the next. These long treks had exhausted him. Cold, frightened, and poorly fed, he had grown very weak.

14 Worst of all had been the ear episode. The kidnappers had tried to knock him out before they cut off his ear. "They struck me on the head to make me unconscious," he said. "But I felt everything. It was terrible."

15 With Paul safe, the police turned their attention to catching the kidnappers. Undercover officers had seen men pick up the ransom money. So the police knew who the kidnappers were.

16 In late January 1974, police made their move. They arrested all eight kidnappers. And so the kidnappers did not get to enjoy much of the Getty money. It had been the highest ransom ever paid in Italy. But as these kidnappers discovered, they had to return the money *and* go to jail.

If you have been timed while reading this article, enter your reading time below. Then turn to the Words-per-Minute Table on page 55 and look up your reading speed (words per minute). Enter your reading speed on the graph on page 56.

Reading Time: Lesson 3

_____ : _____
Minutes   Seconds

A | Finding the Main Idea

One statement below expresses the main idea of the article. One statement is too general, or too broad. The other statement explains only part of the article; it is too narrow. Label the statements using the following key:

M—Main Idea   **B—Too Broad**   **N—Too Narrow**

_____ 1. When the grandson of the world's richest man was kidnapped, the result was pain for the young man but no gain for the kidnappers.

_____ 2. Nobody believed that young John Paul Getty had been kidnapped until the kidnappers sent a newspaper an envelope containing his ear.

_____ 3. As the experience of John Paul Getty III showed, members of rich families are always in danger of kidnapping.

_____ Score 15 points for a correct M answer.

_____ Score 5 points for each correct B or N answer.

_____ **Total Score:** Finding the Main Idea

B | Recalling Facts

How well do you remember the facts in the article? Put an X in the box next to the answer that correctly completes each statement about the article.

1. The kidnappers of John Paul Getty III
   □ a. demanded a ransom of $17 million.
   □ b. sent a ransom note to his grandfather.
   □ c. threatened the Italian government.

2. Police doubted the kidnapping was real because
   □ a. the ransom note looked like a fake.
   □ b. young Getty had been sighted around town.
   □ c. young Getty had joked about faking his own kidnapping.

3. At first, the only person who agreed to pay the ransom was
   □ a. John Paul Getty, Sr.
   □ b. John Paul Getty, Jr.
   □ c. the mother of John Paul Getty III.

4. Later, Paul's family agreed to pay
   □ a. less than $3 million in ransom.
   □ b. what the kidnappers asked at.
   □ c. anything the kidnappers wanted.

5. After the ransom was paid,
   □ a. Paul escaped from his kidnappers.
   □ b. the kidnappers freed Paul.
   □ c. the police freed Paul from the kidnappers.

Score 5 points for each correct answer.

_____ **Total Score:** Recalling Facts

C | Making Inferences

When you combine your own experience with information from a text to draw a conclusion that is not directly stated in that text, you are making an inference. Below are five statements that may or may not be inferences based on information in the article. Label the statements using the following key:

C—Correct Inference   **F—Faulty Inference**

_____ 1. Even members of rich families do not get to spend money as they like.

_____ 2. Paul's jokes about staging his own kidnapping probably gave the idea to the kidnappers.

_____ 3. Kidnappers may settle for a smaller ransom than they first demand.

_____ 4. If Paul Getty had tried to escape, he could have gotten away from his kidnappers easily.

_____ 5. It was only through chance, not ability, that the police caught the kidnappers of Paul Getty.

Score 5 points for each correct answer.

_____ **Total Score:** Making Inferences

D | Using Words Precisely

Each numbered sentence below contains an underlined word or phrase from the article. Following the sentence are three definitions. One definition is closest to the meaning of the underlined word. One definition is opposite or nearly opposite. Label those two definitions using the following key; do not label the remaining definition.

C—Closest   **O—Opposite or Nearly Opposite**

1. Italian police thought it was a hoax.

_____ a. lie

_____ b. adventure

_____ c. reality

2. Police had reasons to be dubious.

_____ a. trusting

_____ b. displeased

_____ c. suspicious

3. All he had to do was stage his own "perfect kidnapping."

_____ a. fake

_____ b. observe

_____ c. arrange

4. When employees opened it, they found a gruesome sight.

_____ a. pretty

_____ b. grisly

_____ c. familiar

5. These long <u>treks</u> had exhausted him.

_____ a. tales

_____ b. waits

_____ c. journeys

Enter the four total scores in the spaces below, and add them together to find your Reading Comprehension Score. Then record your score on the graph on page 57.

Author's Approach

Put an X in the box next to the correct answer.

1. The authors use the first sentence of the article to

☐ a. give the reader a hint about where the kidnapping took place.

☐ b. describe the qualities of police.

☐ c. entertain the reader with a joke.

2. What do the authors mean by the statement "[Paul's] idea of a tough day was going to a big party"?

☐ a. Paul was shy and hated going to big parties.

☐ b. Paul didn't do much work and he partied a great deal.

☐ c. Paul thought that giving a party was a tough job.

3. The authors probably wrote this article to

☐ a. persuade readers not to kidnap anyone.

☐ b. show how rich the Getty family was.

☐ c. inform readers about a famous crime.

4. The authors tell this story mainly by

☐ a. comparing different topics.

☐ b. telling about events in the order they happened.

☐ c. using his or her imagination and creativity.

Summarizing and Paraphrasing

Follow the directions provided for questions 1 and 2. Put an X in the box next to the correct answer for question 3.

1. Complete the following one-sentence summary of the article using the lettered phrases from the phrase bank below. Write the letters on the lines.

Phrase Bank

a. the Getty family's efforts to get Paul released

b. the arrest of the kidnappers

c. Getty's family receiving a ransom note

The article "Kidnapped!" begins with _____, goes on to

explain _____, and ends with _____.

2. Reread paragraph 13 in the article. Below, write a summary of the paragraph in no more than 25 words.

_____

_____

_____

_____

Reread your summary and decide whether it covers the important ideas in the paragraph. Next, decide how to shorten the summary to 15 words or less without leaving out any essential information. Write this summary below.

_____

_____

_____

3. Read the statement about the article below. Then read the paraphrase of that statement. Choose the reason that best tells why the paraphrase does not say the same thing as the statement.

Statement: Paul's mother wanted to ransom Paul, but she did not have enough money, since she was divorced from John Paul Getty, Jr.

Paraphrase: Gail Getty didn't have enough money to ransom Paul because she was divorced from John Paul Getty, Jr.

☐ a. Paraphrase says too much.

☐ b. Paraphrase doesn't say enough.

☐ c. Paraphrase doesn't agree with the statement.

_____ Number of correct answers

Record your personal assessment of your work on the Critical Thinking Chart on page 58.

Critical Thinking

Follow the directions provided for questions 1, and 3. Put an X in the box next to the correct answer for the other questions.

1. For each statement below, write O if it expresses an opinion or write F if it expresses a fact.

_____ a. Paul Getty will never forget his ordeal with the kidnappers.

_____ b. Getty family members did not like young Paul.

_____ c. The kidnappers were given $2.8 million to release Paul.

2. Judging by the events in the article, you can conclude that the

☐ a. Getty family forgave the kidnappers and made sure they didn't spend much time in jail.

☐ b. kidnappers were released from jail very quickly, since they released Paul as they said they would.

☐ c. kidnappers had to spend a long time in jail.

3. Choose from the letters below to correctly complete the following statement. Write the letters on the lines.

In the article, _____ and _____ are alike.

a. old Mr. Getty's feelings about paying a ransom

b. Gail Getty's feelings about paying a ransom

c. the attitude of John Paul Getty, Jr., about paying a ransom

4. How is "Kidnapped!" related to the theme of *Crime and Punishment?*

☐ a. John Paul Getty III was a rich young man who was kidnapped.

☐ b. The kidnappers committed a crime, and they were put in jail for it.

☐ c. Italian police did not take the crime seriously for a while.

_____ Number of correct answers

Record your personal assessment of your work on the Critical Thinking Chart on page 58.

Personal Response

I can't believe _____

_____

_____

_____

Self-Assessment

I'm proud of how I answered question _____ in the _____

section because _____

_____

_____

_____

The Brink's Robbery

Joseph "Big Joe" McGinnis dreamed of committing the perfect crime. In 1948 he hooked up with Tony "Fats" Pino. Pino shared McGinnis's dream. Together, these two longtime criminals set to work. They spent two years planning a flawless robbery. Nothing would be left to chance. No evidence would be left behind. And, if all went well, they would both end up rich.

2   The two thieves picked a tough target to rob—the Brink's Company in Boston. Brink's is an armored car service. It sends steel-plated cars to pick up money from stores around

Brink's armored trucks such as this one, filled with cash on the way to vaults, have been the targets of many robbers. But one gang didn't stop at just the money in a single truck. They went straight to Brink's headquarters.

town. The armored cars take the money to Brink's headquarters. There it is counted, sorted, and held until the stores need it again. In 1950, as much as $10 million a day flowed through the Brink's office.

3   McGinnis and Pino planned their robbery with great care. They picked nine other men to join them. These were not just any nine men. Each brought a special skill to the group. Some, for instance, were good drivers or sharp lookout men. Also, seven of the men had to be the same size. McGinnis and Pino chose men who were about five feet nine inches tall and weighed between 170 and 180 pounds. These men would be the ones to enter the Brink's office and bring out the money. They would all dress alike. They would wear the same scary masks, rubber-soled shoes, gloves, coats, and caps. That would make it hard for the Brink's guards to identify them. (McGinnis would be one of the seven, but Pino was too heavy for the job. He agreed to stay with the getaway truck.)

4   Robbing the Brink's headquarters would not be easy. The place was full of steel vaults and armed guards.

McGinnis and Pino knew this. So they took plenty of time. They studied the layout of the building. They found out when the guards were on duty and where they were stationed. They watched the money flow in and out of the office. They knew when the big money was there.

5   One of the toughest problems they faced was the locks. The gang had to pass through five locked doors to get from the street to the Brink's office. McGinnis and Pino came up with a bold plan. Late one night, a few of the gang members slipped into the building. One of them, a professional locksmith, removed the lock on the first door. He took it away and quickly made a key for it. Then—that same night—he hurried back to the Brink's building. He got the lock back in place before anyone noticed it was missing.

6   The robbers returned on four other nights. Each time they repeated their actions. They made keys for the locks on the four other doors. Now they would be able to walk right into the Brink's office. There, they knew, they would find guards standing inside a wire cage. That was where all the money was.

7   Next, McGinnis and Pino made the gang practice the robbery. More than 20 times, the thieves slipped into the building. They used their keys to unlock door after door. Each time, they got right up to the innermost door. Then they turned and left.

8   At last, McGinnis and Pino decided they were ready for the real thing. On January 17, 1950, they gave the signal. That night, a little before seven o'clock, the men took their places. Seven of them put on masks and sneaked into the building. They opened the five locked doors. At 7:10 p.m., they opened the innermost door. They were in the Brink's office. There, as expected, they saw five guards. The guards were all inside the wire cage, counting money.

9   The thieves stuck their guns through the holes in the cage. "This is a stickup," one growled. "Open the gate and don't give us any trouble." Thomas Lloyd, the head guard, looked at the seven drawn guns. He knew it was hopeless to put up a fight. He instructed one of the other guards to go ahead and open the cage door.

10 Inside the cage, the thieves ordered the guards to lie facedown on the floor. They tied the guards' hands behind their backs. In addition, they tied their feet together and put tape across their mouths. Then the crooks grabbed the money. They took all they could carry.

In total, they stole more than 1,200 pounds in coins, bills, and checks. By 7:27 p.m. they were out of the building. The robbery had gone perfectly. In cash alone, they had made off with exactly $1,218,211.29!

11 When news of the heist spread, people were stunned. They hadn't thought anyone would ever dare rob Brink's. But, clearly, someone had. The police had no clues about who had done it. They searched everywhere. They organized a huge manhunt, but they didn't even know whom they were looking for. All they knew for sure was that the seven robbers were "of medium weight and height."

12 Meanwhile, the Brink's robbers played it safe. They drove the loot to the home of Jazz Maffie in nearby Roxbury. Then each man went back home to his family. The next day they all went to their regular day jobs as if nothing had happened. The thieves stayed calm. They waited a month before splitting up the money. Each man got about $100,000.

13 For six years, the police tried to solve the crime. They failed. But during that time, trouble was brewing inside the gang. One of the robbers did not like the way the money had been divided. Specs O'Keefe began demanding a larger share of the loot. McGinnis and the others became

worried. They feared O'Keefe might go to the police. So they hired a gunman named Trigger Burke to kill him. One day Burke opened fire as O'Keefe drove by in his car. Luckily for O'Keefe—and unluckily for the rest of the gang— Burke missed his target.

14 Furious about the attack, O'Keefe did turn to the police. He told them the whole story. The police quickly rounded up all the Brink's robbers. The 11 men were brought to trial in 1956. All of them, including Specs O'Keefe, were found guilty. Since O'Keefe had helped solve the crime, however, police allowed him to go free. The rest of the gang got long prison terms. In the end, then, the dream of Big Joe McGinnis and Fats Pino had turned into a nightmare.

If you have been timed while reading this article, enter your reading time below. Then turn to the Words-per-Minute Table on page 55 and look up your reading speed (words per minute). Enter your reading speed on the graph on page 56.

Reading Time: Lesson 4

———— : ————

Minutes   Seconds

A Finding the Main Idea

One statement below expresses the main idea of the article. One statement is too general, or too broad. The other statement explains only part of the article; it is too narrow. Label the statements using the following key:

M—Main Idea   **B—Too Broad**   **N—Too Narrow**

_____ 1. The Brink's robbery took a long time to plan.

_____ 2. The Brink's robbery is famous because it took great planning and the robbers left no clues.

_____ 3. To help with their robbery, McGinnis and Pino chose skilled men of average height and weight.

_____ Score 15 points for a correct M answer.

_____ Score 5 points for each correct B or N answer.

_____ **Total Score:** Finding the Main Idea

B Recalling Facts

How well do you remember the facts in the article? Put an X in the box next to the answer that correctly completes each statement about the article.

1. The target of the robbery was the Brink's Company in
   ☐ a. New York City.
   ☐ b. Los Angeles.
   ☐ c. Boston.

2. Every day in 1950, the Brink's office handled about
   ☐ a. $1 million.
   ☐ b. $10 million.
   ☐ c. $100 million.

3. Pino did not enter the Brink's office because he was too
   ☐ a. heavy.
   ☐ b. nervous.
   ☐ c. tall.

4. When the thieves opened the innermost door of the Brink's office, they found
   ☐ a. an armored car.
   ☐ b. police waiting for them.
   ☐ c. guards counting the money.

5. Six years after the robbery, Specs O'Keefe wanted
   ☐ a. a bigger share of the money.
   ☐ b. to tell newspaper reporters about his role in the robbery.
   ☐ c. to kill the rest of the robbers.

Score 5 points for each correct answer.

_____ **Total Score:** Recalling Facts

C | Making Inferences

When you combine your own experience with information from a text to draw a conclusion that is not directly stated in that text, you are making an inference. Below are five statements that may or may not be inferences based on information in the article. Label the statements using the following key:

C—Correct Inference   F—Faulty Inference

_____ 1. Joe McGinnis and Tony Pino trusted and worked well with each other.

_____ 2. It would be easier to rob a regular car than it would to rob an armored truck.

_____ 3. The men who took part in the Brink's robbery were impatient and unable to keep a secret.

_____ 4. The guards who did not resist the robbers were cowards.

_____ 5. The robbers could have gotten away with the money even without a getaway vehicle.

Score 5 points for each correct answer.

_____ **Total Score:** Making Inferences

D | Using Words Precisely

Each numbered sentence below contains an underlined word or phrase from the article. Following the sentence are three definitions. One definition is closest to the meaning of the underlined word. One definition is opposite or nearly opposite. Label those two definitions using the following key; do not label the remaining definition.

C—Closest   O—Opposite or Nearly Opposite

1. Together, these two longtime <u>criminals</u> set to work.

_____ a. people who obey the law

_____ b. people who know a lot about crimes

_____ c. people who break laws

2. They spent two years planning a <u>flawless</u> robbery.

_____ a. perfect

_____ b. full of errors

_____ c. difficult

3. Nothing would be left to <u>chance</u>.

_____ a. the last moment

_____ b. luck

_____ c. planning

4. One of them, a <u>professional</u> locksmith, removed the lock on the first door.

_____ a. without skill or experience

_____ b. expert

_____ c. talkative

5. <u>Furious</u> about the attack, O'Keefe did turn to the police.

_____ a. extremely angry

_____ b. surprised

_____ c. happy

_____ Score 3 points for each correct C answer.

_____ Score 2 points for each correct O answer.

_____ **Total Score:** Using Words Precisely

Enter the four total scores in the spaces below, and add them together to find your Reading Comprehension Score. Then record your score on the graph on page 57.

Score	Question Type	Lesson 4
_____	Finding the Main Idea	
_____	Recalling Facts	
_____	Making Inferences	
_____	Using Words Precisely	
_____	**Reading Comprehension Score**	

Author's Approach

Put an X in the box next to the correct answer.

1. The main purpose of the first paragraph is to
   - ☐ a. describe the steps in the robbery plan.
   - ☐ b. compare Big Joe McGinnis and Fats Pino.
   - ☐ c. emphasize how well the robbery was planned.

2. From the statements below, choose those that you believe the authors would agree with.
   - ☐ a. The robbers were careful and patient.
   - ☐ b. Brink's guards were surprised when the robbers walked in.
   - ☐ c. The police were close to identifying the robbers even before Specs O'Keefe told them the whole story.

3. Choose the statement below that is the weakest argument for becoming a robber.
   - ☐ a. Robbing could make you rich.
   - ☐ b. Robbers run the risk of being killed.
   - ☐ c. Robbers run the risk of being arrested and put in jail.

4. The authors probably wrote this article to
   - ☐ a. tell an interesting story about a famous robbery.
   - ☐ b. teach readers how to become robbers.
   - ☐ c. show how security measures have changed since 1950.

_____ Number of correct answers

Record your personal assessment of your work on the Critical Thinking Chart on page 58.

Summarizing and Paraphrasing

Follow the directions provided for questions 1 and 2. Put an X in the box next to the correct answer for question 3.

1. Complete the following one-sentence summary of the article using the lettered phrases from the phrase bank below. Write the letters on the lines.

> ### Phrase Bank
> a. the robbers' division of the loot, their disagreements, and their arrest and punishment
> b. what happened during the robbery
> c. the preparation for the robbery

The article "The Brink's Robbery" begins with _____, goes

on to explain _____, and ends with _____.

2. Reread paragraph 12 in the article. Below, write a summary of the paragraph in no more than 25 words.

_____

_____

_____

_____

Reread your summary and decide whether it covers the important ideas in the paragraph. Next, decide how to shorten the summary to 15 words or less without leaving out any essential information. Write this summary below.

_____

_____

_____

3. Choose the best one-sentence paraphrase for the following sentence from the article: "Since O'Keefe had helped solve the crime, however, police allowed him to go free."

☐ a. Because he had helped them, the police did not put O'Keefe in jail.

☐ b. O'Keefe was set free because he had not been part of the crime.

☐ c. After O'Keefe solved the crime, the police let him go free.

> _____ Number of correct answers
>
> Record your personal assessment of your work on the Critical Thinking Chart on page 58.

Critical Thinking

Follow the directions provided for questions 1 and 4. Put an X in the box next to the correct answer for question 3.

1. For each statement below, write O if it expresses an opinion or write F if it expresses a fact.

_____ a. McGinnis and Pino deserved to succeed in their robbery because they were so careful and patient.

_____ b. The robbery took place on January 17, 1950.

_____ c. Police were unable to solve the Brink's case for six years.

2. From what the article told about the Brink's security system, you can predict that

☐ a. Brink's kept the system exactly the same after the robbery.

☐ b. Brink's improved their security system after the robbery.

☐ c. after the robbery, Brink's decided that security systems don't work anyway, so they would not bother with a security system anymore.

3. Choose from the letters below to correctly complete the following statement. Write the letters on the lines.

In the article, _____ and _____ are different.

a. how Specs O'Keefe felt about his split of the loot

b. how Big Joe McGinnis felt about his split of the loot

c. how Tony Pino felt about his split of the loot

4. Reread paragraph 13. Then choose from the letters below to correctly complete the following statement. Write the letters on the lines.

According to paragraph 13, _____ because _____

a. the police were not able to solve the crime for six years

b. the robbers were afraid that Specs O'Keefe would tell the police who had committed the robbery

c. the robbers hired a gunman to kill Specs O'Keefe

_____ Number of correct answers

Record your personal assessment of your work on the Critical Thinking Chart on page 58.

Personal Response

What would you have done if you had been one of the workers counting the money and the robbers with guns had surprised you?

_____

_____

_____

_____

Self-Assessment

When I was reading the article, I was having trouble with _____

_____

_____

_____

Dumb Criminals

Who's smarter—the police or the crooks? If you judge by what you see in the movies or on TV, it's the crooks. They always seem to be one step ahead of the cops. The police, on the other hand, are often portrayed as bungling fools. In real life, however, it's not like that. In real life, crooks are some of the dumbest people around. Here are a few of their stories.

2   A young man in Flint, Michigan, walked into a gas station wearing a hooded mask. He pulled out a gun and told the clerk to hand over the money.

This photo could function as an idiot's guide to how to get caught in the act. Real-life stories about the mistakes that criminals make on the job prove that many lawbreakers are not geniuses, to say the least.

The clerk obeyed and the thief quickly ran off with the cash. There was just one problem. The robber was wearing his high school jacket. On it, bold letters spelled out his school, his class year, and his *name*! By the time the young robber got home, the cops were waiting.

3   Then there was the case of the car thief in Knox County, Tennessee. When he was brought into court, the judge asked him how he was going to plead: guilty or not guilty. It was a simple question. But the thief didn't limit his answer to one of those two choices. "Before we go any further, Judge," he said, "let me explain why I stole the car."

4   Many crooks prefer to strike at night. They don't want to risk being seen in broad daylight. Also, it's usually easier to get away in the dark. But that was not the case for one thief in Lawrence, Kansas. The man robbed an all-night market at gunpoint. After stuffing the loot into his pants, he fled on foot. Local cops rushed to the scene. Two officers saw the man as he ran behind some houses. They chased after him, but the crook ran too fast and knew the neighborhood too well.

He soon lost the pursuing cops.

5   The thief felt sure he was safe, but he was wrong. Soon another cop was on his tail. Once more, the thief fled. He eluded this third cop, but then a fourth cop appeared. The robber outran one cop after another, but each time a new police officer would take up the chase. The crook couldn't understand how they kept picking up his trail.

6   At last, the police cornered him. There were simply too many of them. It was only then that the crook discovered his mistake. The high-tech sneakers he was wearing had red lights in the heels. Each time he took a step, the lights flashed. So the police had had no trouble at all seeing him in the dark.

7   Anyone would like to win the lottery. But most people who play it lose. Losing is one thing. But losing by one lousy number is something else. One Oregon woman couldn't stand the thought that she had *almost* won. Then she had an idea. What if she took a ballpoint pen and changed one wrong number into one right number? Then she would have a winning ticket worth $20.

8   The woman just couldn't resist the temptation. She used her pen to alter

the number. Then she went to a clerk to cash in the ticket. Unfortunately for her, she wasn't a good forger. The clerk saw the change and called the police. As the woman was being taken away, one police officer found out how dumb she really was. He could see the real number under the ink mark. True, it wasn't a $20 winner. It was a $5,000 winner!

9 Then there was the man who decided to rob a California branch of the Bank of America. On the back of a deposit slip, he wrote a note. It said he was holding up the bank and wanted all the money put in a bag. But as the man waited in line to hand the slip to a teller, he grew nervous. What if someone had seen him writing the note? Maybe someone had already called the cops. The would-be crook lost his nerve and walked out of the bank.

10 He then spied a branch of the Wells Fargo Bank on the other side of the street. Why not rob it instead? So he waited in line at that bank. He handed his note to a Wells Fargo teller. As the teller read it, she saw that it had lots of spelling errors. Figuring this crook was not very bright, she told him that she could not accept the note because it was written on a Bank of America slip. She said the man would have to write a new stickup note on a Wells Fargo slip. Or he could go back to the Bank of America and use his original stickup note there.

11 The man looked disappointed. But he said, "OK." Then he walked out of the bank. Quickly the teller called the police. Officers came and arrested the man as he stood in line at the Bank of America.

12 One of the dumbest criminals of all time has to be the young man who tried to rob a grocery store in San Francisco. Holding a shotgun, the man told the clerk to give him all the cash. The clerk put the money in a bag. But before he could hand it over, the crook spotted a bottle of whiskey on a shelf. Pointing to the bottle, he said, "Put that in the bag too."

13 The clerk refused. He reminded the robber that the legal drinking age was 21—and he didn't think the robber was that old. The robber insisted that he was over 21. The clerk still shook his head. So the robber said, "I'll prove it. Here's my license."

14 The clerk looked at the license and agreed that indeed the robber was old enough to drink. The clerk put the whiskey in the bag along with the money from the cash register. After the thief took off with the bag, the clerk called the police. He gave them the crook's name and address, both of which he had gotten from the driver's license. A few hours later, the cops arrested the crook.

15 The list of inept criminals goes on and on. In one case, a man was charged with stealing money from vending machines. He paid his $400 bail with quarters.

16 Another man ran into a police station shouting, "This is a stickup." He had meant to rob the post office next door.

17 Then there was the guy who asked a clerk to change a $20 bill. When the clerk opened up the register, the crook demanded all the cash. There was only $8 in the till. The crook grabbed the money and ran away. He left his $20 behind. And people wonder why the prisons are overcrowded.

A Finding the Main Idea

One statement below expresses the main idea of the article. One statement is too general, or too broad. The other statement explains only part of the article; it is too narrow. Label the statements using the following key:

M—Main Idea   **B—Too Broad**   **N—Too Narrow**

_____ 1. Crooks can be foolish.

_____ 2. Many criminals make foolish mistakes that make them easy to catch and punish.

_____ 3. One of many examples of dumb criminals is the young robber who left behind a $20 bill and got away with only $8.

_____ Score 15 points for a correct M answer.

_____ Score 5 points for each correct B or N answer.

_____ **Total Score:** Finding the Main Idea

B Recalling Facts

How well do you remember the facts in the article? Put an X in the box next to the answer that correctly completes each statement about the article.

1. Police were able to follow the robber of an all-night market in the dark because
   ☐ a. his sneakers had red lights.
   ☐ b. he was wearing his school jacket.
   ☐ c. he was nervous.

2. A man who had written a holdup note on a bank deposit slip went to another bank because he
   ☐ a. had no account at the first bank.
   ☐ b. was afraid someone had seen him write the note and had called the cops.
   ☐ c. decided there was more money at the second bank.

3. One woman changed a number on what she thought was
   ☐ a. a bank deposit slip.
   ☐ b. her driver's license.
   ☐ c. a losing lottery ticket.

4. A robber at a grocery store tripped up when he
   ☐ a. ran into the police station next door.
   ☐ b. took off his school jacket.
   ☐ c. showed his driver's license to a clerk to prove he was over 21.

5. The man who paid his $400 bail in quarters was accused of
   ☐ a. stealing money from a vending machine.
   ☐ b. robbing a bank.
   ☐ c. robbing an all-night market.

Score 5 points for each correct answer.

_____ **Total Score:** Recalling Facts

49

C | Making Inferences

When you combine your own experience with information from a text to draw a conclusion that is not directly stated in that text, you are making an inference. Below are five statements that may or may not be inferences based on information in the article. Label the statements using the following key:

C—Correct Inference   **F—Faulty Inference**

_____ 1. When the judge asked the car thief how he was pleading, he was trying to trick the thief into confessing.

_____ 2. If the thief with the red lights in his sneakers had worn shoes without lights, he would have been harder to follow.

_____ 3. The woman who changed the number on her lottery ticket was a careless reader.

_____ 4. All criminals make foolish, careless mistakes every time they commit a crime.

_____ 5. People who are being robbed are always so upset that they can't think straight.

Score 5 points for each correct answer.

_____ **Total Score:** Making Inferences

D | Using Words Precisely

Each numbered sentence below contains an underlined word or phrase from the article. Following the sentence are three definitions. One definition is closest to the meaning of the underlined word. One definition is opposite or nearly opposite. Label those two definitions using the following key; do not label the remaining definition.

C—Closest   **O—Opposite or Nearly Opposite**

1. The police, on the other hand, are often <u>portrayed</u> as bungling fools.

_____ a. rewarded

_____ b. pictured

_____ c. ignored

2. Unfortunately, she wasn't a very good <u>forger</u>.

_____ a. person who refuses to change a document illegally

_____ b. person who notices that a document has been changed

_____ c. person who changes a document illegally

3. The list of <u>inept</u> criminals goes on and on.

_____ a. foolish and incompetent

_____ b. skillful

_____ c. desperate

4. Or he could go back to the Bank of America and use his <u>original</u> stickup note there.

_____ a. fake

_____ b. first

_____ c. new

5. Pointing to the bottle, he said, "Put that in the bag too." The clerk <u>refused</u>.

_____ a. said no

_____ b. laughed

_____ c. agreed

_____ Score 3 points for each correct C answer.

_____ Score 2 points for each correct O answer.

_____ **Total Score:** Using Words Precisely

Enter the four total scores in the spaces below, and add them together to find your Reading Comprehension Score. Then record your score on the graph on page 57.

Score	Question Type	Lesson 5
_____	Finding the Main Idea	
_____	Recalling Facts	
_____	Making Inferences	
_____	Using Words Precisely	
_____	**Reading Comprehension Score**	

Author's Approach

Put an X in the box next to the correct answer.

1. The main purpose of the first paragraph is to

☐ a. persuade the reader not to watch TV.

☐ b. tell the main idea of the article.

☐ c. point out how smart police officers are.

2. What is the authors' purpose in writing "Dumb Criminals"?

☐ a. to entertain the reader with funny stories

☐ b. to persuade the reader to respect police officers

☐ c. to inform the reader about serious crimes and the way criminals are punished

3. What do the authors imply by saying "In one case, a man was charged with stealing money from vending machines. He paid his $400 bail in quarters"?

☐ a. The man was poor.

☐ b. The man was probably a coin collector.

☐ c. The man was probably guilty because he had so many coins that people put in vending machines.

4. The authors tell this story mainly by

☐ a. retelling personal experiences that happened to them.

☐ b. using their imagination and creativity.

☐ c. telling different stories about the same topic.

_____ Number of correct answers

Record your personal assessment of your work on the Critical Thinking Chart on page 58.

Summarizing and Paraphrasing

Follow the directions provided for question 1. Put an X in the box next to the correct answer for question 2.

1. Look for the important ideas and events in paragraphs 7 and 8. Summarize those paragraphs in one or two sentences.

_____

_____

_____

2. Read the statement about the article below. Then read the paraphrase of that statement. Choose the reason that best tells why the paraphrase does not say the same thing as the statement.

   Statement: One crook tried to rob a Wells Fargo Bank using a note on the back of a Bank of America deposit slip.

   Paraphrase: One crook robbed a Bank of America branch using a Wells Fargo deposit slip.

   ☐ a. Paraphrase says too much.

   ☐ b. Paraphrase doesn't say enough.

   ☐ c. Paraphrase doesn't agree with the statement.

   _____ Number of correct answers

   Record your personal assessment of your work on the Critical Thinking Chart on page 58.

Critical Thinking

Put an X in the box next to the correct answer for questions 1, 2, 4, and 5. Follow the directions provided for question 3.

1. Which of the following statements from the article is an opinion rather than a fact?

   ☐ a. The high-tech sneakers he was wearing had red lights in the heels.

   ☐ b. One of the dumbest criminals of all time has to be the young man who tried to rob a grocery store in San Francisco.

   ☐ c. Many crooks prefer to strike at night.

2. From what the article told about the case in which a man mistook the police station for a post office he wanted to rob, you can predict that after he yelled, "This is a stickup,"

   ☐ a. he was arrested.

   ☐ b. the police officers directed him to the post office next door.

   ☐ c. he felt embarrassed and left quickly.

3. Reread paragraph 2. Then choose from the letters below to correctly complete the following statement. Write the letters on the lines.

   According to paragraph 2, _____ because _____.

   a. he had personal information in bold letters on the jacket he was wearing

   b. he wore a hooded mask

   c. the young man was arrested for robbing a gas station

4. How is "Dumb Criminals" related to the theme of *Crime and Punishment?*

☐ a. The criminals made silly mistakes when they committed their crimes.

☐ b. The criminals showed that they were not very smart.

☐ c. All the criminals were caught and punished.

5. What did you have to do to answer question 3?

☐ a. find an opinion (what someone thinks about something)

☐ b. find an effect (something that happened)

☐ c. find a cause (why something happened)

_____ Number of correct answers

Record your personal assessment of your work on the Critical Thinking Chart on page 58.

Personal Response

Would you recommend this article to other students? Explain.

_____

_____

_____

_____

Self-Assessment

Which concepts or ideas from the article were difficult to understand?

_____

_____

_____

Which were easy?

_____

_____

_____

Compare and Contrast

Think about the articles you have read in Unit One. Pick the three most dangerous criminals. Write the titles of the articles in the first column of the chart below. Use information you learned from the articles to fill in the empty boxes in the chart.

Title	What personal qualities made these criminals especially dangerous?	What crimes did the criminals commit?	What weapons were used in the crimes?

The criminal I think was most dangerous was _____. I chose this criminal because

_____

_____

Words-per-Minute Table

Unit One

Directions: If you were timed while reading an article, refer to the Reading Time you recorded in the box at the end of the article. Use this words-per-minute table to determine your reading speed for that article. Then plot your reading speed on the graph on page 56.

Lesson No. of Words	Sample 644	1 1,112	2 839	3 870	4 1,066	5 1,125	Seconds
1:30	429	741	559	580	711	750	90
1:40	386	667	503	522	640	675	100
1:50	351	607	458	475	581	614	110
2:00	322	556	420	435	533	563	120
2:10	297	513	387	402	492	519	130
2:20	276	477	360	373	457	482	140
2:30	258	445	336	348	426	450	150
2:40	242	417	315	326	400	422	160
2:50	227	392	296	307	376	397	170
3:00	215	371	280	290	355	375	180
3:10	203	351	265	275	337	355	190
3:20	193	334	252	261	320	338	200
3:30	184	318	240	249	305	321	210
3:40	176	303	229	237	291	307	220
3:50	168	290	219	227	278	293	230
4:00	161	278	210	218	267	281	240
4:10	155	267	201	209	256	270	250
4:20	149	257	194	201	246	260	260
4:30	143	247	186	193	237	250	270
4:40	138	238	180	186	228	241	280
4:50	133	230	174	180	221	233	290
5:00	129	222	168	174	213	225	300
5:10	125	215	162	168	206	218	310
5:20	121	209	157	163	200	211	320
5:30	117	202	153	580	194	205	330
5:40	114	196	148	154	188	199	340
5:50	110	191	144	149	183	193	350
6:00	107	185	140	145	178	188	360
6:10	104	180	136	141	173	182	370
6:20	102	176	132	522	168	178	380
6:30	99	171	129	134	164	173	390
6:40	97	167	126	131	160	169	400
6:50	94	163	123	127	156	165	410
7:00	92	159	120	124	152	161	420
7:10	90	155	117	121	149	157	430
7:20	88	152	114	119	145	153	440
7:30	86	148	112	116	142	150	450
7:40	84	145	109	113	139	147	460
7:50	82	142	107	111	136	144	470
8:00	81	139	105	109	133	141	480

Minutes and Seconds

Plotting Your Progress: Reading Speed

Unit One

Directions: If you were timed while reading an article, write your words-per-minute rate for that article in the box under the number of the lesson. Then plot your reading speed on the graph by putting a small X on the line directly above the number of the lesson, across from the number of words per minute you read. As you mark your speed for each lesson, graph your progress by drawing a line to connect the X's.

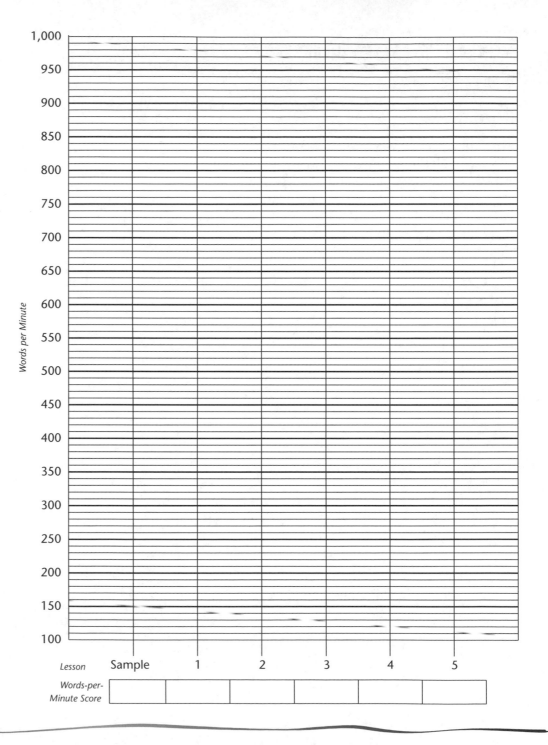

Plotting Your Progress: Reading Comprehension

Unit One

Directions: Write your Reading Comprehension score for each lesson in the box under the number of the lesson. Then plot your score on the graph by putting a small X on the line directly above the number of the lesson and across from the score you earned. As you mark your score for each lesson, graph your progress by drawing a line to connect the X's.

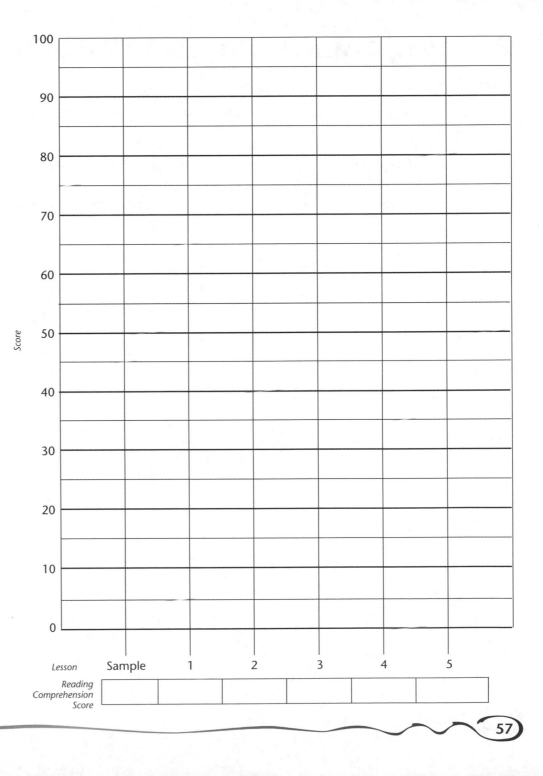

Lesson	Sample	1	2	3	4	5
Reading Comprehension Score						

Plotting Your Progress: Critical Thinking

Unit One

Directions: Work with your teacher to evaluate your responses to the Critical Thinking questions for each lesson. Then fill in the appropriate spaces in the chart below. For each lesson and each type of Critical Thinking question, do the following: Mark a minus sign (–) in the box to indicate areas in which you feel you could improve. Mark a plus sign (+) to indicate areas in which you feel you did well. Mark a minus-slash-plus sign (–/+) to indicate areas in which you had mixed success. Then write any comments you have about your performance, including ideas for improvement.

Lesson	Author's Approach	Summarizing and Paraphrasing	Critical Thinking
Sample			
1			
2			
3			
4			
5			

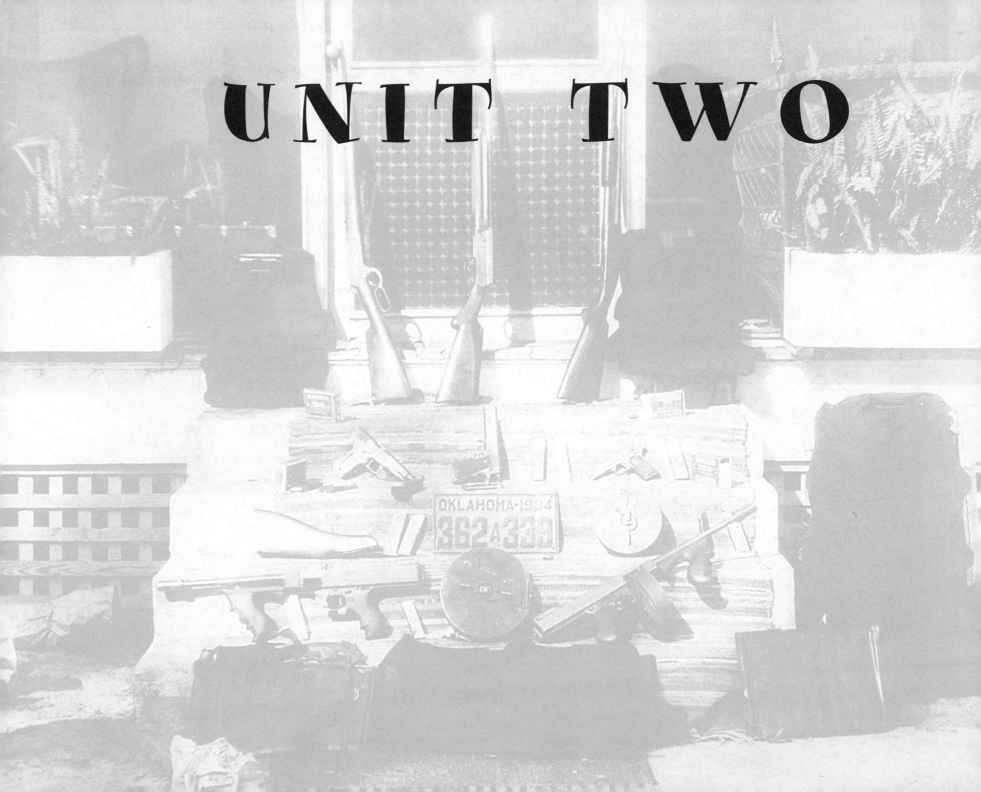

UNIT TWO

The Real Jesse James

Jesse James is often pictured as a kind of modern-day Robin Hood. People talk about how he stole from the rich and gave to the poor. There have been songs, books, and movies about his heroic nature. But the real Jesse James was no hero. He was nothing but a thief and a killer.

2   Jesse Woodson James was born near Kearny, Missouri, in 1847. At the age of 15, he went to war. He fought on the side of the South in the Civil War. He was not, however, a regular soldier. Jesse joined a gang of raiders led by the cruel William Quantrill.

All of these men appear to be upstanding citizens. However, looks can be deceiving. This is the James gang, a group of notorious bandits and killers in the Old West.

They attacked and burned the homes of people who sided with the North. When the Civil War ended in 1865, the raiders broke up. Jesse and his older brother, Frank, went back to their farms.

3   No one knows for sure why Jesse and Frank turned to a life of crime. But they did. Maybe, after the thrill of war, farming seemed pretty dull. Jesse himself later blamed Northerners. He claimed Northerners who had taken over local banks refused to give loans to Southern farmers like himself. "We were driven to it," Jesse said. But that was a weak excuse. Jesse James didn't care about the fate of Southern farmers. After all, most of the people whom he robbed and killed were Southerners. There is no evidence that he ever gave a dime of stolen money to the poor—or to anyone else.

4   Early in 1866, Jesse became a member of an outlaw gang. His brother Frank was in the gang. So were several other old Quantrill raiders. On February 13, 1866, the gang robbed its first bank. The outlaws rode into Liberty, Missouri, in the middle of the day. A few went into the bank. They threatened to blow the bank teller's head off unless he gave them all the money.

5   Meanwhile, the other gang members kept watch outside. After the robbery, the outlaws jumped on their horses and headed out of town. In the street, they passed a college student named George Wymore. He was on his way to class. Seeing the riders thundering down the street, Wymore ran for cover. One of the gang members shot him in the back. He died instantly. It was the first of many times an innocent person was gunned down by this gang. Jesse soon showed he was the most daring of the gang members and the most willing to kill. People began to think of him as the gang's leader.

6   After each bank robbery, Jesse and the rest of the gang went into hiding. They waited for the public outrage to die down. It was usually many months before they hit another bank. Sometimes they passed the time by ambushing stagecoaches and robbing the passengers. Then, in 1873, the James gang found a much richer target—trains. That year they planned their first train robbery. They picked the Rock Island Express in Adair, Iowa. Jesse and the other men stopped the train by taking away a piece of the track. When engineer John Rafferty saw the broken track, he threw his engine into reverse. It was too late. The train crashed onto its side, killing Rafferty. James and his gang made off with about $2,000.

7   By 1874 Jesse James was world famous. He added to his fame with the boldest train robbery up to that time. It took place in the small town of Gad's Hill, Missouri. Not only did Jesse's gang steal all the train's money, but they robbed everyone on board as well. The outlaws loved every minute of it. One grabbed the hat off a passenger's head. Another laughingly told a minister on board to pray for them. Jesse even wrote his own news story about the crime. He left it with a passenger, saying, "Give that to the editor of the *St. Louis Dispatch*." Since he hadn't counted the money yet, Jesse left a blank space for the amount of money stolen.

8   Jesse planned each raid carefully. He and his men struck by surprise.

Often they met little or no resistance. That was because these former Civil War raiders knew how to terrorize people. Still, that did not always work. Sometimes the townspeople fought back. One day the gang tried to rob a bank in Savannah, Missouri. Led by a local judge, the citizens drove them away before the outlaws got a nickel. The gang later robbed a bank in Richmond, Missouri. The citizens there formed a posse to chase them. The posse caught three of the robbers and lynched them from a nearby tree.

9   In 1876 the gang was nearly destroyed when the members tried to rob a bank in Northfield, Minnesota. Again they ran into some tough townsfolk. The outlaws tried to scare people by firing shots in the air. They hoped to stir up enough panic so they could make a clean getaway. But the townspeople knew what the gunshots meant. The bank was being robbed! Several citizens sprang into action. They grabbed their guns and took off after the gang. Only Jesse and Frank managed to escape. All the rest of the gang members were captured or killed.

10   Shaken, Jesse and Frank went into hiding. For weeks they dared travel only at night. They slept in barns and stayed alive by eating raw vegetables from the fields. For three years they kept a low profile. They waited for a chance to resume their life of crime.

11   At last, in 1879, Jesse put together a new gang. The robbing and killing began all over again. By this time, many people had had enough of Jesse. The reward for his capture or death kept mounting. Lots of people wanted to collect the reward. Jesse knew he had to be extra careful now.

12   Every member of the gang felt the pressure. Lawmen might be lurking behind any tree. They might be waiting around any corner. One gang member, Ed Miller, asked Jesse to give up. Jesse responded by shooting him. As it turned out, Jesse killed the wrong man. It was gang member Bob Ford who soon turned against Jesse. Ford went to see the governor of Missouri. No one ever found out what the governor promised him, but it must have been good. On April 3, 1882, Ford went to see Jesse at his cabin near St. Joseph, Missouri. While Jesse's back was turned, Ford pulled out his gun. He shot Jesse James in the back of the head. Some people were saddened by Jesse's death. But others were pleased to see the end of America's most famous outlaw.

If you have been timed while reading this article, enter your reading time below. Then turn to the Words-per-Minute Table on page 101 and look up your reading speed (words per minute). Enter your reading speed on the graph on page 102.

Reading Time: Lesson 6

_____ : _____
Minutes   Seconds

A Finding the Main Idea

One statement below expresses the main idea of the article. One statement is too general, or too broad. The other statement explains only part of the article; it is too narrow. Label the statements using the following key:

M—Main Idea   **B—Too Broad**   **N—Too Narrow**

_____ 1. Jesse James was a clever but heartless killer who led gangs in bank and train robberies until he was killed by one of his own men for a reward.

_____ 2. Jesse James, a famous outlaw, was one of the many lawless men who roamed the American West after the Civil War.

_____ 3. After most of his gang was caught or killed following an 1876 bank robbery, Jesse James hid for three years before resuming his life of crime.

_____ Score 15 points for a correct M answer.

_____ Score 5 points for each correct B or N answer.

_____ **Total Score:** Finding the Main Idea

B Recalling Facts

How well do you remember the facts in the article? Put an X in the box next to the answer that correctly completes each statement about the article.

1. During the Civil War, Jesse James fought
   ☐ a. in the infantry of the Union army.
   ☐ b. in the Confederate cavalry, under Sherman.
   ☐ c. for the South, with Quantrill's raiders.

2. Jesse's gang began by robbing
   ☐ a. stagecoaches.
   ☐ b. trains.
   ☐ c. banks.

3. In the James gang's first train robbery, the engineer was killed
   ☐ a. in the train wreck that the gang caused.
   ☐ b. by gunfire when the gang attacked.
   ☐ c. when he refused to cooperate.

4. When the James gang left the Missouri area to rob a bank in Minnesota, the Minnesota townspeople
   ☐ a. caught or killed all but the James brothers.
   ☐ b. were too frightened to resist.
   ☐ c. were happy to have a famous outlaw visit.

5. Jesse died
   ☐ a. while running from a bungled bank job.
   ☐ b. while at home in Missouri.
   ☐ c. by hanging after a short trial.

Score 5 points for each correct answer.

_____ **Total Score:** Recalling Facts

C Making Inferences

When you combine your own experience and information from a text to draw a conclusion that is not directly stated in that text, you are making an inference. Below are five statements that may or may not be inferences based on information in the article. Label the statements using the following key:

C—Correct Inference   **F—Faulty Inference**

_____ 1. Many legends about so-called heroes of the American West have little connection with the facts.

_____ 2. After the Civil War, most former Confederate soldiers turned to lives of crime.

_____ 3. Jesse James and his gang enjoyed getting publicity for their crimes.

_____ 4. In small towns of the late 1800s, citizens relied entirely on their police forces to maintain order.

_____ 5. Some members of Jesse's second, or new, gang did not really respect or admire Jesse.

Score 5 points for each correct answer.

_____ **Total Score:** Making Inferences

D Using Words Precisely

Each numbered sentence below contains an underlined word or phrase from the article. Following the sentence are three definitions. One definition is closest to the meaning of the underlined word. One definition is opposite or nearly opposite. Label those two definitions using the following key; do not label the remaining definition.

C—Closest   **O—Opposite or Nearly Opposite**

1. There have been songs, books, and movies about his heroic nature.

_____ a. brave and noble

_____ b. cowardly

_____ c. stylish

2. For three years they kept a low profile.

_____ a. showed off

_____ b. behaved quietly so as to avoid notice

_____ c. stayed on a diet

3. The reward for his capture or death kept mounting.

_____ a. calling

_____ b. falling

_____ c. rising

4. He and his men struck by surprise. Often they met little or no resistance.

_____ a. giving in

_____ b. ability

_____ c. opposition

5. They hoped to stir up enough <u>panic</u> so they could make a clean getaway.

_____ a. interest

_____ b. sudden, widespread terror

_____ c. calmness

_____ Score 3 points for each correct C answer.

_____ Score 2 points for each correct O answer.

_____ **Total Score:** Using Words Precisely

Enter the four total scores in the spaces below, and add them together to find your Reading Comprehension Score. Then record your score on the graph on page 103.

Score	Question Type	Lesson 6
_____	Finding the Main Idea	
_____	Recalling Facts	
_____	Making Inferences	
_____	Using Words Precisely	
_____	**Reading Comprehension Score**	

Author's Approach

Put an X in the box next to the correct answer.

1. The main purpose of the first paragraph is to

☐ a. explain why Jesse James is famous.

☐ b. reveal Jesse James's true nature.

☐ c. describe the way Jesse James robbed from the rich and gave to the poor.

2. Which of the following statements from the article best describes the way Jesse James committed his crimes?

☐ a. Early in 1866, Jesse became a member of an outlaw gang.

☐ b. He [Jesse] fought on the side of the South in the Civil War.

☐ c. Jesse planned each raid carefully. He and his men struck by surprise.

3. Choose the statement below that best explains how the authors address the opposing point of view in the article.

☐ a. The authors point out that some people picture Jesse James as a hero.

☐ b. The authors explain that Jesse James blamed Northerners for his life of crime.

☐ c. The authors point out that Jesse James was shot in the back by one of his own men.

_____ Number of correct answers

Record your personal assessment of your work on the Critical Thinking Chart on page 103.

Summarizing and Paraphrasing

Follow the directions provided for question 1. Put an X in the box next to the correct answer for question 2.

1. Reread paragraph 9 in the article. Below, write a summary of the paragraph in no more than 25 words.

_____

_____

_____

Reread your summary and decide whether it covers the important ideas in the paragraph. Next, decide how to shorten the summary to 15 words or less without leaving out any essential information. Write this summary below.

_____

_____

_____

2. Read the statement about the article below. Then read the paraphrase of that statement. Choose the reason that best tells why the paraphrase does not say the same thing as the statement.

Statement: Jesse and his gang robbed trains and their passengers during the times when they were not robbing banks.

Paraphrase: In between bank robberies, Jesse and his gang committed smaller crimes, such as ambushing stagecoaches and robbing the passengers.

☐ a. Paraphrase says too much.

☐ b. Paraphrase doesn't say enough.

☐ c. Paraphrase doesn't agree with the statement about the article.

_____ Number of correct answers

Record your personal assessment of your work on the Critical Thinking Chart on page 104.

Critical Thinking

Put an X in the box next to the correct answer for questions 1, 2, 3, and 4. Follow the directions provided for question 5.

1. Which of the following statements from the article is an opinion rather than a fact?

☐ a. James and his gang made off with about $2,000.

☐ b. Early in 1866, Jesse became a member of an outlaw gang.

☐ c. No one ever found out what the governor promised [Bob Ford], but it must have been good.

2. Considering Bob Ford's actions as described in this article, you can predict that after he shot Jesse James, he

☐ a. received a nice reward from the governor.

☐ b. felt sad and regretful.

☐ c. was congratulated by the other gang members.

3. What was the effect of the outlaws firing shots into the air in Northfield, Minnesota, during a bank robbery?

☐ a. The townspeople became frightened.

☐ b. The townspeople realized that the bank was being robbed and chased after the robbers.

☐ c. Some members of the James gang were hit by falling bullets.

4. Of the following theme categories, which would this story fit into?

☐ a. You can trust people you work with.

☐ b. Criminals would rather not break the law; they are forced into lives of crime.

☐ c. There is no honor among thieves.

5. In which paragraph did you find your information or details to answer question 3? _____

_____ Number of correct answers

Record your personal assessment of your work on the Critical Thinking Chart on page 104.

Personal Response

I agree with the author that Jesse James was no hero because

_____

_____

_____

_____

Self-Assessment

One good question about this article that was not asked would be

_____

_____

and the answer is ___ _____

_____

_____

Typhoid Mary

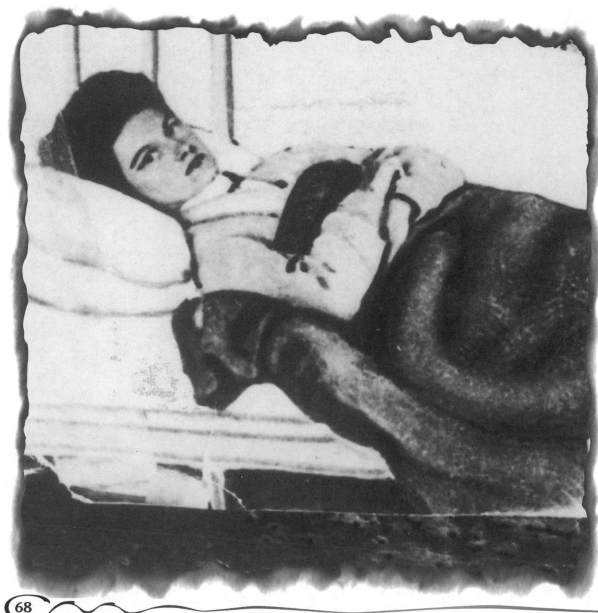

Mary Mallon didn't mean to kill people. For a long time, she didn't even realize she was doing it. All she knew was that wherever she went, people got sick. It was a pattern. She would be hired as a cook by a wealthy New York family. She would begin making meals. But within weeks, the family would come down with a horrible disease called *typhoid*.

2   The disease began with chills and a fever. Victims often felt sick to their stomach. They developed a headache

Confined in a hospital for testing, Mary Mallon glares defiantly at the camera. This seemingly healthy woman never believed what the medical tests revealed—that she was the carrier of typhoid bacteria that killed many people who ate her cooking.

and suffered from nosebleeds. Next, they broke out with a bright red rash.They began coughing. Sometimes the fever would break and they would recover. In other cases, their condition would worsen and they would die.

3   In the early 1900s few people understood how typhoid is spread. Some people thought it came from spoiled milk. Others thought it came from garbage fumes. Only a few scientists had figured out the truth: it is caused by germs that live inside the human body. These germs pass through the body when a person uses the toilet. Sometimes the germs get on a person's hands. If the person touches food before washing up, the germs can be transferred to the food. Anyone who eats the food can then come down with the disease. In the early 1900s, about one out of every five people sick with typhoid died.

4   Mary Mallon had never had typhoid. She had always been healthy and strong. She had no reason to think she might be passing the disease on to anyone. And yet . . . no matter where she went, typhoid soon followed. Mary's reaction to this problem was

simple. She ran away. Once she did stay and help nurse a family through the illness. But the rest of the time, she just packed her bags and moved on.

5   In 1906 Mary got a job as the cook for Charles Warren and his family. She had been with the Warrens just three weeks when one of the children got a fever. Mary knew what that meant. Typhoid had struck again. Quickly she collected her pay. Then she took off. But this time she was followed. A man named George Soper began investigating the Warren family's illness.

6   Soper was an expert on diseases. He knew how typhoid was spread. He figured that healthy people could carry typhoid germs around without knowing it. Perhaps, he thought, Mary Mallon was a carrier of these germs. He decided to track her down. He wanted to run tests to see if her body housed typhoid germs.

7   Soper found Mary in March of 1907. She was working as a cook for yet another New York family. As Soper had feared, a girl in the house was already dying of typhoid. Soper went to the house. Mary was in the kitchen.

When Soper told her why he had come, she became furious. She picked up a huge carving fork and lunged at him. Soper managed to run away without being hurt.

8   Soon after that, Soper went to see where Mary lived. It was a dirty, smelly place. Standing in the filth, Soper understood how Mary could spread typhoid to so many people. She clearly had very poor health habits.

9   Soper sent Dr. Josephine Baker to talk to Mary. Baker worked for the city. It was her job to protect people from health hazards. But Baker had no luck, either. Mary simply did not believe what the doctor told her. It sounded crazy. After all, she was healthy. Surely she was not carrying typhoid around inside her body. Mary just wanted everyone to leave her alone. She wanted to go on earning a living as a cook. And as for washing her hands after using the toilet—well, that seemed like a waste of time and energy.

10   Baker and other city officials did not know what to do. At last they decided to lock Mary up. It was a desperate move. But no one could think of any other way to stop her

from spreading typhoid. Baker and five police officers went to get her. When Mary saw them coming, she fled. After a two-hour search, she was found crouching in a neighbor's yard. When the police grabbed her, she began kicking and biting. It took all five officers to drag her into an ambulance. Said Dr. Baker, "I literally sat on her all the way to the hospital. It was like being in a cage with an angry lion."

11 Mary was kept at the hospital for months. As expected, tests showed that her body was full of typhoid germs. That fall, she was transferred to a hospital on a tiny island near the city. She was kept there for three years. She got a lawyer to help her fight for her freedom. She argued that it was illegal for the city to hold her prisoner. Mary was right, but no judge was willing to set her free. And so she remained locked up on North Brother Island.

12 In 1910 Mary finally agreed to do what the doctors wanted. If they let her go, she said, she would never work as a cook again. She also promised to check in with them every three months. Doctors agreed to the plan. They turned Mary loose. But as soon as she was back on the streets, she vanished. For five years, no city official could find her.

13 During that time, Mary floated from one restaurant job to the next. She cooked for hotels. She cooked in diners. She made up different names for herself. And she ran away whenever one of her customers got typhoid.

14 In 1915 Mary got a kitchen job at the Sloane Hospital for Women in New York City. Soon 25 people there came down with typhoid. One of the workers joked that the cook must be the infamous Typhoid Mary. Terrified of being caught again, Mary took off for New Jersey. But now police were on her trail. On May 27, 1915, she was arrested and returned to North Brother Island.

15 Mary Mallon had reached the end of the line. Health officials were not going to give her any more chances.

They decided to keep her on that little island for the rest of her life. For 22 years, until her death at age 70, that's where Mary stayed. In her later years, she was given her own cottage to live in. She could have visitors whenever she wanted. At mealtime, though, everyone knew what to do. They always left without eating a bite of Typhoid Mary's cooking.

If you have been timed while reading this article, enter your reading time below. Then turn to the Words-per-Minute Table on page 101 and look up your reading speed (words per minute). Enter your reading speed on the graph on page 102.

Reading Time: Lesson 7

_____ : _____
Minutes   Seconds

A Finding the Main Idea

One statement below expresses the main idea of the article. One statement is too general, or too broad. The other statement explains only part of the article; it is too narrow. Label the statements using the following key:

M—Main Idea   **B—Too Broad**   **N—Too Narrow**

_____ 1. George Soper was the first person to suspect that Mary Mallon might have caused the Warren family's illness.

_____ 2. Typhoid is a powerful disease that can cause grave illness and even death.

_____ 3. Mary Mallon carried deadly typhoid germs and infected many victims before she was arrested and put in a hospital.

_____ Score 15 points for a correct M answer.

_____ Score 5 points for each correct B or N answer.

_____ **Total Score:** Finding the Main Idea

B Recalling Facts

How well do you remember the facts in the article? Put an X in the box next to the answer that correctly completes each statement about the article.

1. Mary Mallon cooked for wealthy families in
   - ☐ a. New York City.
   - ☐ b. Pennsylvania.
   - ☐ c. Florida.

2. Typhoid germs are carried around in
   - ☐ a. spoiled milk.
   - ☐ b. the human body.
   - ☐ c. garbage fumes.

3. Usually, when Mary's victims became ill, she
   - ☐ a. reported their illness to health officials.
   - ☐ b. nursed them back to health.
   - ☐ c. packed her bags and left.

4. It was hard for Mary to believe that she could spread typhoid because she
   - ☐ a. could not understand what typhoid was.
   - ☐ b. was very healthy herself.
   - ☐ c. did not even know that her victims were getting sick.

5. To get released, Mary agreed never to
   - ☐ a. work as a cook again.
   - ☐ b. make her home in New York City.
   - ☐ c. leave the United States.

Score 5 points for each correct answer.

_____ **Total Score:** Recalling Facts

C | Making Inferences

When you combine your own experience and information from a text to draw a conclusion that is not directly stated in that text, you are making an inference. Below are five statements that may or may not be inferences based on information in the article. Label the statements using the following key:

C—Correct Inference   **F—Faulty Inference**

_____ 1. Mary Mallon was a gentle, honest person who would go to great lengths not to harm anyone.

_____ 2. In the early 1900s wealthy people often hired cooks to prepare their meals in their homes.

_____ 3. It is a good idea to make sure that all workers in restaurants wash their hands after they use the toilet.

_____ 4. As long as you feel healthy and strong, you can never be a carrier of typhoid germs.

_____ 5. Mary Mallon had extraordinary strength, especially when she was upset or angry.

Score 5 points for each correct answer.

_____ **Total Score:** Making Inferences

D | Using Words Precisely

Each numbered sentence below contains an underlined word or phrase from the article. Following the sentence are three definitions. One definition is closest to the meaning of the underlined word. One definition is opposite or nearly opposite. Label those two definitions using the following key; do not label the remaining definition.

C—Closest   **O—Opposite or Nearly Opposite**

1. Standing in the <u>filth</u>, Soper understood how Mary could spread typhoid to so many people.

_____ a. dirt

_____ b. purity

_____ c. room

2. Sometimes the fever would break and they would <u>recover</u>.

_____ a. become pale

_____ b. get back to normal

_____ c. worsen

3. All she knew was that wherever she went, people got sick. It was a <u>pattern</u>.

_____ a. arrangement by chance

_____ b. worry

_____ c. set of repeating events or items

4. But as soon as she was back on the streets, she <u>vanished</u>.

_____ a. understood

_____ b. disappeared

_____ c. reappeared

5. She picked up a huge carving fork and <u>lunged at</u> him.

_____ a. backed away from

_____ b. attacked

_____ c. shouted at

_____ Score 3 points for each correct C answer.

_____ Score 2 points for each correct O answer.

_____ **Total Score:** Using Words Precisely

Enter the four total scores in the spaces below, and add them together to find your Reading Comprehension Score. Then record your score on the graph on page 103.

Score	Question Type	Lesson 7
_____	Finding the Main Idea	
_____	Recalling Facts	
_____	Making Inferences	
_____	Using Words Precisely	
_____	**Reading Comprehension Score**	

Author's Approach

Put an X in the box next to the correct answer.

1. What is the authors' purpose in writing "Typhoid Mary"?

☐ a. to encourage the reader to cook his or her own food

☐ b. to inform the reader about advances in medicine

☐ c. to describe a strange situation in which a woman killed others without meaning to

2. Judging by statements from the article "Typhoid Mary," you can conclude that the authors want the reader to think that

☐ a. Mary would have followed good health rules if they had been explained to her clearly.

☐ b. health officials were cruel and unfair in dealing with Mary.

☐ c. the only way to protect the public was to keep Mary locked up.

3. What do the authors imply by saying "[The guests] always left without eating a bit of Typhoid Mary's cooking"?

☐ a. Guests were afraid that Mary could still pass on typhoid germs in her cooking.

☐ b. Mary really disliked cooking and never offered guests anything to eat.

☐ c. Health officials would not permit Mary to have any food in her cottage.

_____ Number of correct answers

Record your personal assessment of your work on the Critical Thinking Chart on page 104.

Summarizing and Paraphrasing

Follow the directions provided for questions 1 and 2. Put an X in the box next to the correct answer for question 3.

1. Look for the important ideas and events in paragraphs 8 and 9. Summarize those paragraphs in one or two sentences.

_____

_____

_____

2. Complete the following one-sentence summary of the article using the lettered phrases from the phrase bank below. Write the letters on the lines.

> ### Phrase Bank
> a. a description of typhoid fever
> b. the way that officials stopped Mary from giving anyone the typhoid fever
> c. how officials figured out that Mary Mallon was passing on typhoid fever

The article "Typhoid Mary" begins with _____, goes on to

explain _____, and ends with _____.

3. Choose the sentence that correctly restates the following passage from the article: "Soper sent Dr. Josephine Baker to talk to Mary. Baker worked for the city. It was her job to protect people from health hazards."

☐ a. Mary went to Dr. Josephine Baker and Soper to discuss health hazards. She worked for the city.

☐ b. Soper asked Mary to visit Dr. Josephine Baker, who worked for the city. She was in charge of health protection.

☐ c. At Soper's request, Dr. Josephine Baker visited Mary. The doctor, who worked for the city, tried to protect people from health hazards.

_____ Number of correct answers

Record your personal assessment of your work on the Critical Thinking Chart on page 104.

Critical Thinking

Put an X in the box next to the correct answer for the following questions.

1. From the article, you can predict that if Mary had been released, she would have

☐ a. stopped cooking for a living.

☐ b. changed her cooking and washing habits.

☐ c. gone back to cooking and not washing her hands.

2. What was the cause of Mary's employers' typhoid fever?

☐ a. Mary passed on typhoid germs from her unwashed hands.

☐ b. Typhoid germs from the garbage Mary refused to clean up got into her cooking.

☐ c. Mary used spoiled milk that contained typhoid germs.

3. If you were a restaurant owner, how could you best use the information in the article to serve safe food to your customers?

☐ a. You could keep track of how many of your customers got typhoid fever.

☐ b. You could demand that people who handle food wash their hands after using the toilet.

☐ c. You could do all the cooking and serving by yourself.

4. What did you have to do to answer question 2?

☐ a. find an opinion (what someone thinks about something)

☐ b. find a description (how something looks)

☐ c. make a comparison (how things are the same)

_____ Number of correct answers

Record your personal assessment of your work on the Critical Thinking Chart on page 104.

Personal Response

This article is different from other articles about crime and punishment I've read because _____

_____

_____

_____

and Mary Mallon is unlike other killers because _____

_____

_____

_____

Self-Assessment

I can't really understand how _____

_____

_____

_____

How Bad Was Ma Barker?

Was she "Bloody Mama"? Or was she just plain Mom? Was she the brains who planned all the bank robberies and murders? Or was she just a doting mother who never thought her sons did anything wrong? If you believe the movies and the FBI, Kate "Ma" Barker was bad, really bad. But if you believe the gang members, "The old woman couldn't plan breakfast."

The FBI believed Ma Barker was the brains behind an unusual family business— robbing, murdering, and kidnapping. Some of the gang's weapons are shown here on the porch of the family hideout.

2 Kate was still a teenager when she married George Barker in 1892. He was a poor farmer with no ambition. It was not a happy marriage. Still, the Barkers had four boys—Herman, Lloyd, Doc, and Freddie. The Barkers moved around a lot, living in one tarpaper shack after another. George was almost worthless as a father. When his rowdy boys got into trouble with his neighbors, he shrugged. "You'll have to talk to Mother," he would say. "She handles the boys."

3 Ma Barker had a different response to the neighbors. When they accused her sons of some prank, she lashed out. She screamed and called them liars. Her sons were innocent—always.

4 As the Barker brothers grew older they moved up the ladder of crime. At first they were petty thieves. When the cops arrested them, Ma came to the rescue. She cried, begged, and pleaded with the police to let her boys go. Many times, that's what they did.

5 In the late 1910s the boys began robbing banks. The FBI said Ma Barker planned the robberies. They said she told the boys what to do. She even checked out all the getaway routes. She knew how long it would take to escape on this road or that road. She knew how much more time would be needed if it rained. According to the FBI, Ma ruled her boys with an iron fist. Although she never robbed any banks in person, she was the brilliant mind behind all the crimes.

6 That is one version of Ma Barker.

7 The other version comes from members of the gang. The Barker brothers often joined up with other hoods. One was Alvin "Creepy" Karpis. He said Ma didn't do a thing. The gang planned everything when she wasn't around. "It's no insult to Ma's memory," Karpis later wrote, "that she just didn't have the brains or know-how to direct us. We'd leave her at home when we were arranging a job, or we'd send her to a movie. Ma saw a lot of movies."

8 While people argue about Ma Barker's true role, no one disputes what her boys did. They conducted their own personal crime wave. They robbed banks and trains. In time, they added murder and kidnapping to their list of felonies.

9 One by one, the sons paid for their crimes. Lloyd was tried and found guilty of mail robbery. The judge gave him 25 years in prison. (When he got out of prison, Lloyd gave up his life of crime. He served in the Army during World War II. Even so, he came to a violent end. His wife shot and killed him in 1949.)

10 Herman also died a violent death. On August 1, 1927, he shot and killed a police officer after robbing a bank. Four weeks later, Ma's boy shot another cop. He and two other gang members had just robbed a store. In the gun battle with police, Herman was shot but not killed. Seeing no way out, he turned his gun on himself and took his own life. According to the FBI, Herman's death turned Ma Barker into a "beast of prey." In her grief, she ruled the gang with even harsher authority.

11 If Ma did indeed become heartless, that would have been just fine with Doc. He was the most ruthless of all the brothers. Once, when the gang wanted one of its own members killed, Doc quickly volunteered. He shot the man in a barn. Then he soaked everything in gasoline and set the barn on fire. Later Doc bragged about the killing. In a note he wrote

to some of the other gang members, he said, "I took care of that business for you boys. It was done just as good as if you did it yourself. Always at your service. Ha, ha!"

12 In 1922 Doc was convicted for killing a night watchman during one of the gang's robberies. The court sentenced him to life in prison. He was later given a pardon. The governor of Oklahoma told him to get out of the state and never come back. But Doc couldn't stay out of trouble. Soon he was back in prison. On January 13, 1939, Doc tried to escape. The guards saw him and opened fire. Badly wounded, Doc was taken back to prison. He died the next day.

13 By 1935 Ma and Freddie were the only Barkers still free. That was about to end. Ma and her youngest son were hiding out in Florida. The FBI was after them for kidnapping. A tip led federal agents to a cottage at Lake Weir. Early on January 16, agents surrounded the cottage. They called for the Barkers to toss out their guns and come out with their hands up. Freddie gave his answer with a burst of machine gun fire.

14 The ensuing battle lasted for four hours. Each side fired away for about 15 minutes. Then there was a period of silence. That was followed by another round of gunfire. "It was like war," said a woman who lived across from the Barkers. "I was suddenly awakened by guns firing. I got out of bed, and as I stood up some bullets came through the closed door." The woman and her daughter climbed out a back window and ran for safer ground.

15 At last, around 11 A.M., the firing stopped for good. One man went into the house to check out the scene. He soon reappeared. "They are all dead," he said.

16 Freddie had been shot more than a dozen times. Ma Barker had just one bullet in her. The agents reported that she went down with "a machine gun in her hands." But was she shot by an agent's bullet or did she kill herself? Some people think that she shot herself in despair after Freddie died. No one knows for sure.

17 With her death, the FBI turned Ma Barker into a legend. As far as the world was concerned, she was "Bloody Mama." Many people called her Public Enemy Number One. Hollywood shared this view. A movie about her life shows her being shot with a blazing machine gun in her hands. But was she really an outlaw or just the mother of outlaws? Today many experts have their doubts. They think the gang members were telling the truth when they said Ma Barker was clueless. They think that perhaps Kate Barker was just a mom—a bad mom— but still just a mom. 🐾

If you have been timed while reading this article, enter your reading time below. Then turn to the Words-per-Minute Table on page 101 and look up your reading speed (words per minute). Enter your reading speed on the graph on page 102.

Reading Time: Lesson 8

———— : ————
Minutes   Seconds

A Finding the Main Idea

One statement below expresses the main idea of the article. One statement is too general, or too broad. The other statement explains only part of the article; it is too narrow. Label the statements using the following key:

M—Main Idea   **B—Too Broad**   **N—Too Narrow**

_____ 1. The Barker family was responsible for robberies, murders, and kidnapping, but no one knows for sure what Ma Barker's role was in their crime spree.

_____ 2. Ma Barker and her family became famous during the early years of the 20th century.

_____ 3. The four boys in the famous Barker family were Herman, Lloyd, Doc, and Freddie.

_____ Score 15 points for a correct M answer.

_____ Score 5 points for each correct B or N answer.

_____ **Total Score:** Finding the Main Idea

B Recalling Facts

How well do you remember the facts in the article? Put an X in the box next to the answer that correctly completes each statement about the article.

1. The Barker boys' father, George, was a
   ☐ a. petty criminal.
   ☐ b. farmer.
   ☐ c. restaurant owner.

2. The FBI believed that Ma Barker was
   ☐ a. the organizer of the Barker family crimes.
   ☐ b. innocent of all crimes.
   ☐ c. upset that her boys were criminals and anxious for them to turn themselves in.

3. Herman died a violent death in 1927 when
   ☐ a. his wife killed him.
   ☐ b. police killed him in a gun battle.
   ☐ c. he committed suicide during a gun battle with police.

4. Doc was killed by
   ☐ a. prison guards after he tried to escape.
   ☐ b. the guards at a bank he was robbing.
   ☐ c. the wife of a man he had shot.

5. One crime that no member of the Barker family committed was
   ☐ a. robbery.
   ☐ b. kidnapping.
   ☐ c. hijacking a plane.

Score 5 points for each correct answer.

_____ **Total Score:** Recalling Facts

C | Making Inferences

When you combine your own experience with information from a text to draw a conclusion that is not directly stated in that text, you are making an inference. Below are five statements that may or may not be inferences based on information in the article. Label the statements using the following key:

C—Correct Inference   **F—Faulty Inference**

_____ 1. At the time Ma Barker was shot, police couldn't know for sure which gun a bullet had been fired from.

_____ 2. If George Barker had been a better father, his boys would never have gotten into trouble with the law.

_____ 3. Ma Barker loved her children.

_____ 4. The Barker family worked together on every crime they committed.

_____ 5. Planning a successful robbery requires care and intelligence.

Score 5 points for each correct answer.

_____ **Total Score:** Making Inferences

D | Using Words Precisely

Each numbered sentence below contains an underlined word or phrase from the article. Following the sentence are three definitions. One definition is closest to the meaning of the underlined word. One definition is opposite or nearly opposite. Label those two definitions using the following key; do not label the remaining definition.

C—Closest   **O—Opposite or Nearly Opposite**

1. Or was she just a <u>doting</u> mother who never thought her sons did anything wrong?

_____ a. cold

_____ b. extremely affectionate

_____ c. young

2. Although people argue about Ma Barker's true role, no one <u>disputes</u> what her boys did.

_____ a. denies

_____ b. praises

_____ c. agrees

3. In time, they added murder and kidnapping to their list of <u>felonies</u>.

_____ a. awards

_____ b. small crimes

_____ c. major crimes

4. The court sentenced him to life in prison. He was later given a <u>pardon</u>.

_____ a. an official penalty for a crime

_____ b. an official document that takes away a penalty for a crime

_____ c. jail cell

5. The <u>ensuing</u> battle lasted for four hours.

_____ a. long

_____ b. following

_____ c. coming before; preceding

_____ Score 3 points for each correct C answer.

_____ Score 2 points for each correct O answer.

_____ **Total Score:** Using Words Precisely

Enter the four total scores in the spaces below, and add them together to find your Reading Comprehension Score. Then record your score on the graph on page 103.

Score	Question Type	Lesson 8
_____	Finding the Main Idea	
_____	Recalling Facts	
_____	Making Inferences	
_____	Using Words Precisely	
_____	**Reading Comprehension Score**	

Author's Approach

Put an X in the box next to the correct answer.

1. Which two of the following statements from the article best describe the FBI's view of Ma Barker?

☐ a. Although she never robbed any banks in person, she was the brilliant mind behind all the crimes.

☐ b. In her grief, she ruled the gang with even harsher authority.

☐ c. The gang planned everything when she wasn't around.

2. In this article, "[Ma Barker's] sons were innocent—always." means

☐ a. Ma Barker was not realistic about her sons' behavior.

☐ b. the Barker boys really never did anything wrong when they were young.

☐ c. the Barker boys always acted innocent even when they were guilty.

3. How is the authors' purpose for writing the article expressed in paragraph 17?

☐ a. This paragraph stresses that Ma Barker has become a legend.

☐ b. This paragraph states that many people called Ma Barker Public Enemy Number One.

☐ c. This paragraph repeats the question about Ma Barker's role in her family's crimes.

_____ Number of correct answers

Record your personal assessment of your work on the Critical Thinking Chart on page 104.

Summarizing and Paraphrasing

Follow the directions provided for question 1. Put an X in the box next to the correct answer for question 2.

1. Reread paragraph 11 in the article. Below, write a summary of the paragraph in no more than 25 words.

_____

_____

_____

Reread your summary and decide whether it covers the important ideas in the paragraph. Next, decide how to shorten the summary to 15 words or less without leaving out any essential information. Write this summary below.

_____

_____

_____

2. Read the statement about the article below. Then read the paraphrase of that statement. Choose the reason that best tells why the paraphrase does not say the same thing as the statement.

Statement: During a gun battle with the FBI, Ma Barker may have shot herself after seeing that her son Freddie had been killed.

Paraphrase: It is possible that Ma Barker committed suicide during a gun battle with the FBI.

☐ a. Paraphrase says too much.

☐ b. Paraphrase doesn't say enough.

☐ c. Paraphrase doesn't agree with the statement about the article.

_____ Number of correct answers

Record your personal assessment of your work on the Critical Thinking Chart on page 104.

Critical Thinking

Follow the directions provided for questions 1 and 2. Put an X in the box next to the correct answer for the other questions.

1. Choose from the letters below to correctly complete the following statement. Write the letters on the lines.

In the article, _____ and _____ are alike.

a. the way that Lloyd died

b. the way that Ma Barker may have died

c. the way that Herman died

2. Think about cause-effect relationships in the article. Fill in the blanks in the cause-effect chart, drawing from the letters below.

Cause	Effect
Ma Barker pleaded with the police.	_____
Ma Barker was in charge of the boys' discipline.	_____
_____	Ma Barker saw a lot of movies.

a. The gang didn't want Ma Barker around when they planned crimes.

b. The police often let the Barker boys go after they were caught stealing.

c. People with complaints about the boys had to talk to Ma Barker.

3. Of the following theme categories, which would this story fit into?

☐ a. No matter what you choose to do, throw all your energy into your job.

☐ b. Defending her family against criticism is the most important job a mother can do.

☐ c. The way people are raised affects their whole lives.

4. What did you have to do to answer question 1?

☐ a. find a comparison (how things are the same)

☐ b. find an opinion (what someone thinks about something)

☐ c. make a prediction (what might happen next)

_____ Number of correct answers

Record your personal assessment of your work on the Critical Thinking Chart on page 104.

Personal Response

What new question do you have about this topic?

_____

_____

_____

Self-Assessment

One of the things I did best when reading this article was _____

_____

_____

I believe I did this well because _____

_____

_____

Dillinger: A Crook with Style

John Dillinger could have done anything he wanted with his life. He was a smart kid with a lot of friends. He had plenty of courage. And he was a terrific athlete. In fact, the governor of Indiana once declared, "That kid ought to be playing major league baseball." But John Dillinger did not become a baseball player or a businessman or a teacher. He became a criminal.

Even crooks need a break now and then. John Dillinger thought so when he took a girlfriend to the movies at this theater in Chicago. He didn't know she had tipped off FBI agents, who waited for him outside.

2   Dillinger was born in Indianapolis, Indiana, in 1903. By the time he got to sixth grade, he was already breaking the law. He stole coal from a railroad yard. Then he sold it to neighbors as heating fuel for their homes.

3   Dillinger got into real trouble when he was 21. He tried to rob an elderly store owner. No one was hurt in the robbery, but Dillinger wound up in police hands. The police encouraged him to plead guilty. They assured him that if he did, the judge would go easy on him. Dillinger took their advice and pleaded guilty. But the judge was in a bad mood that day. He slapped Dillinger with a sentence of 10 to 20 years.

4   The harsh punishment shocked everyone. The store owner himself later asked that the sentence be cut down. Even so, Dillinger served nine years in prison. By the time he got out, he was filled with contempt for the law. Still, from his point of view, the years in prison had not been a total loss. He had become friends with some other convicts. They had taught him everything they knew about robbing banks. When Dillinger was released, he promised not to forget them. He vowed to return and help them escape as soon as he could.

5   First, though, Dillinger needed some cash. So, in the summer of 1933, he robbed a string of banks. Dillinger planned his crimes with great care. He studied the alarm system of each bank. He laid out escape routes and picked good hideouts. But what really set Dillinger apart from other robbers was the style he brought to the job. He would stroll into a bank dressed in a nice suit. Pulling out his gun, he would politely ask the tellers to hand over the money. Often he would leap over a railing or two, moving with an easy grace that impressed everyone. Sometimes he would even flirt with women in the bank. Word of his actions spread quickly. More and more people began to talk about this dashing bank robber named John Dillinger.

6   By September Dillinger had quite a stash of money. True to his word, he remembered his friends back in prison. He arranged to have weapons smuggled in to them. Armed with those weapons, 10 of Dillinger's buddies broke free.

7   Over the next 12 months, Dillinger and this gang of thieves tore across the country. They robbed bank after bank. Sometimes they got just a few thousand dollars. But often they made off with much more. On October 23, 1933, they walked away with more than $75,000. It was Dillinger's biggest haul. It was also the robbery that made him a folk hero in the eyes of many people. Again, it wasn't just what he did—it was the way he did it.

8   On that October day, Dillinger and his men went to Greencastle, Indiana. They entered the Central National Bank. With a gun in his hand, Dillinger made a dramatic leap over a railing. He and his men then stuffed fistfuls of money into their sacks. As they were leaving, Dillinger noticed a man off to the side. He was a farmer who had come to put some money in the bank. His money still lay on the counter in front of a teller's window.

9   Dillinger looked at the stack of bills. "Is that your money or the bank's?" he asked.

10   "Mine," said the farmer.

11 "Keep it," Dillinger told him. "We only want the bank's."

12 It was that kind of remark that made Dillinger famous. Sure, he was a crook, people said. But he was such an *honorable* crook! The police took a different view. They knew Dillinger and his gang had killed several people. The thieves shot anyone who got in their way. More victims could fall any day. So the FBI put Dillinger on their Most Wanted list.

13 Actually, the police got their hands on Dillinger a couple of times. But both times he broke out of jail before a trial could be held. His most spectacular escape came on March 3, 1934. Dillinger had been put in jail in Crown Point, Indiana. Everyone said that jail was escape-proof. Dozens of extra guards were brought in just to make sure of that. Somehow, though, John Dillinger got his hands on a weapon. It is not clear whether he used a real gun or simply a piece of wood shaped like a gun. In any case, it looked real enough to the guards. Dillinger flashed it at them, then escaped down a flight of stairs.

14 By July 1934 Dillinger's gang had stolen more than $250,000. And they had done it in just a few months. But Dillinger's days as a high-flying gangster were coming to an end. According to police, he was betrayed by one of his girlfriends. Anna Sage came to the Chicago police. She offered to take them to Dillinger. In return, they agreed to help her get out of some legal troubles.

15 Police records show that on July 22, Sage went to a movie with Dillinger. She wore a red dress so police agents could spot her in the crowd. When she walked out of the theater with Dillinger, six agents moved in. Sensing trouble, Dillinger whirled and reached for his gun. But the agents were ready. Three of them fired at Dillinger, who dropped to the ground, dead.

16 That is one version of the story. But another version says that it was not John Dillinger who died outside a Chicago theater that day. According to this story, Anna Sage tricked police. She had told them that she would be with Dillinger. However, some people claim, her unfortunate companion was really a small-time crook named Jimmy Lawrence.

17 There are a few facts to support this theory. Doctors who examined the body said the dead man had a damaged heart. Dillinger could not have made his fancy leaps with such a heart. He could never have played baseball, either. Doctors said they found no scars on the dead man. But Dillinger's body should have shown a couple of old bullet wounds. Finally, doctors said the dead man's eyes were brown. Dillinger's were blue.

18 It may be that the doctors were sloppy when they examined Dillinger's body. Or it may be that police shot the wrong man. We'll never know for sure. All we know is this: after July 22, 1934, John Dillinger never bothered anyone again.

If you have been timed while reading this article, enter your reading time below. Then turn to the Words-per-Minute Table on page 101 and look up your reading speed (words per minute). Enter your reading speed on the graph on page 102.

Reading Time: Lesson 9

_____ : _____
Minutes   Seconds

A Finding the Main Idea

One statement below expresses the main idea of the article. One statement is too general, or too broad. The other statement explains only part of the article; it is too narrow. Label the statements using the following key:

M—Main Idea　　**B—Too Broad**　　**N—Too Narrow**

_____ 1. During the 1930s, several criminals caught the attention of the American public.

_____ 2. In his short career in crime, bank robber John Dillinger impressed the public with his daring and style.

_____ 3. According to some sources, John Dillinger once escaped from jail using only a piece of wood shaped like a gun.

_____ Score 15 points for a correct M answer.

_____ Score 5 points for each correct B or N answer.

_____ **Total Score:** Finding the Main Idea

B Recalling Facts

How well do you remember the facts in the article? Put an X in the box next to the answer that correctly completes each statement about the article.

1. John Dillinger first went to jail for
   ☐ a. killing a bank guard.
   ☐ b. stealing a car.
   ☐ c. robbing an elderly store owner.

2. While in jail, Dillinger
   ☐ a. finished high school.
   ☐ b. learned about robbing banks from other convicts.
   ☐ c. had time to plan his escape.

3. In Dillinger's single biggest bank robbery, he stole
   ☐ a. less than $10,000.
   ☐ b. more than $75,000.
   ☐ c. about $1 million.

4. To make sure Dillinger wouldn't escape from the jail at Crown Point, Indiana, officials
   ☐ a. built a special fence.
   ☐ b. put Dillinger in a cell in the basement.
   ☐ c. brought in dozens of extra guards.

5. Police finally gunned down Dillinger as he
   ☐ a. left a movie theater.
   ☐ b. escaped from jail.
   ☐ c. robbed another bank.

Score 5 points for each correct answer.

_____ **Total Score:** Recalling Facts

C | Making Inferences

When you combine your own experience and information from a text to draw a conclusion that is not directly stated in that text, you are making an inference. Below are five statements that may or may not be inferences based on information in the article. Label the statements using the following key:

C—Correct Inference   **F—Faulty Inference**

_____ 1. Dillinger might have led a normal life if he had not been given such a harsh sentence for his first crime.

_____ 2. John Dillinger was an impatient man who could not be bothered with details.

_____ 3. Dillinger was honest in his dealings with his friends.

_____ 4. During the 1930s, newspapers and radio broadcasts never described the details of robberies.

_____ 5. John Dillinger sometimes wore a gun in public even when he was not planning on using it.

Score 5 points for each correct answer.

_____ **Total Score:** Making Inferences

D | Using Words Precisely

Each numbered sentence below contains an underlined word or phrase from the article. Following the sentence are three definitions. One definition is closest to the meaning of the underlined word. One definition is opposite or nearly opposite. Label those two definitions using the following key; do not label the remaining definition.

C—Closest   **O—Opposite or Nearly Opposite**

1. By the time he got out, he was filled with <u>contempt</u> for the law.

_____ a. respect

_____ b. scorn

_____ c. questions

2. When Dillinger was <u>released</u>, he promised not to forget them.

_____ a. set free

_____ b. older

_____ c. imprisoned

3. But he was such an _honorable_ crook!

_____ a. shameful

_____ b. handsome

_____ c. worthy of respect

4. More and more people began to talk about this <u>dashing</u> bank robber named John Dillinger.

_____ a. stylish; showy

_____ b. dull

_____ c. balding

5. His most <u>spectacular</u> escape came on March 3, 1934.

_____ a. comfortable

_____ b. ordinary

_____ c. stunning

_____ Score 3 points for each correct C answer.

_____ Score 2 points for each correct O answer.

_____ **Total Score:** Using Words Precisely

Enter the four total scores in the spaces below, and add them together to find your Reading Comprehension Score. Then record your score on the graph on page 103.

Score	Question Type	Lesson 9
_____	Finding the Main Idea	
_____	Recalling Facts	
_____	Making Inferences	
_____	Using Words Precisely	
_____	**Reading Comprehension Score**	

Author's Approach

Put an X in the box next to the correct answer.

1. The main purpose of the first paragraph is to

☐ a. describe John Dillinger.

☐ b. explain why John Dillinger became a criminal.

☐ c. explain how John Dillinger carried out his robberies.

2. Choose the statement below that is the best argument for believing that someone else was killed in John Dillinger's place.

☐ a. The dead man's eyes were brown, and Dillinger's were blue.

☐ b. His girlfriend loved him too much to betray him.

☐ c. Dillinger was too smart to get caught by the police.

3. Choose the statement below that best describes the authors' position in paragraph 18.

☐ a. The dead man was definitely John Dillinger.

☐ b. The dead man could not have been John Dillinger.

☐ c. It doesn't matter who died that day because Dillinger never committed a crime again.

4. The authors tell this story mainly by

☐ a. telling different stories about the same topic.

☐ b. telling about events in the order they happened.

☐ c. using their imagination and creativity.

_____ Number of correct answers

Record your personal assessment of your work on the Critical Thinking Chart on page 104.

Summarizing and Paraphrasing

Put an X in the box next to the correct answer for questions 1 and 3. Follow the directions provided for question 2.

1. Below are summaries of the article. Choose the summary that says all the most important things about the article but in the fewest words.

☐ a. Although he was a robber and a killer, John Dillinger was admired by many people during the 1930s.

☐ b. John Dillinger became famous for his stylish way of committing crimes during the 1930s. He successfully stole more than $250,000 and his gang killed several people before he was finally shot down by police.

☐ c. John Dillinger started on his career in crime after a judge gave him a harsh sentence for robbing a store. Dillinger broke his gang out of jail and started robbing banks. He was a master at breaking out of jail himself, escaping from a so-called escape-proof jail in 1934.

2. Reread paragraph 12 in the article. Below, write a summary of the paragraph in no more than 25 words.

_____

_____

_____

Reread your summary and decide whether it covers the important ideas in the paragraph. Next, decide how to shorten the summary to 15 words or less without leaving out any essential information. Write this summary below.

_____

_____

_____

3. Read the statement from the article below. Then read the paraphrase of that statement. Choose the reason that best tells why the paraphrase does not say the same thing as the statement.

Statement: Dillinger didn't take one farmer's money during one of his bank robberies.

Paraphrase: During one robbery, Dillinger decided not to take one farmer's money because he said he wanted only the bank's money.

☐ a. Paraphrase says too much.

☐ b. Paraphrase doesn't say enough.

☐ c. Paraphrase doesn't agree with the statement.

_____ Number of correct answers

Record your personal assessment of your work on the Critical Thinking Chart on page 104.

Critical Thinking

Put an X in the box next to the correct answer for questions 1, 4, and 5. Follow the directions provided for the other questions.

1. Which of the following statements from the article is an opinion rather than a fact?

☐ a. But he was such an *honorable* crook!

☐ b. By July 1934 Dillinger's gang had stolen more than $250,000.

☐ c. [The judge] slapped Dillinger with a sentence of 10 to 20 years.

2. Choose from the letters below to correctly complete the following statement. Write the letters on the lines.

In the article, _____ and _____ are different.

a. the jail sentence that young John Dillinger expected to get

b. the jail sentence that young John Dillinger hoped to get

c. the jail sentence that young John Dillinger actually got

3. Read paragraph 14. Then choose from the letters below to correctly complete the following statement. Write the letters on the lines.

According to paragraph 14, Anna Sage _____ because
_____.

a. needed help to get out of legal troubles

b. was one of Dillinger's girlfriends

c. agreed to help police

4. How is "Dillinger: A Crook with Style" related to the theme of *Crime and Punishment*?

☐ a. John Dillinger was athletic and stylish, and many people admired him.

☐ b. John Dillinger was a robber and a killer who paid for his crimes with his death.

☐ c. John Dillinger seemed more honorable than most criminals.

5. What did you have to do to answer question 2?

☐ a. find an opinion (what someone thinks about something)

☐ b. find a description (how something looks)

☐ c. find a contrast (how things are different)

_____ Number of correct answers

Record your personal assessment of your work on the Critical Thinking Chart on page 104.

Personal Response

How do you think Anna Sage felt when the police killed the man thought to be John Dillinger?

_____

_____

_____

_____

Self-Assessment

While reading the article, I found it easiest to _____

_____

_____

_____

Assassin!

On April 4, 1968, Dr. Martin Luther King, Jr., went to Memphis, Tennessee. He checked into the Lorraine Motel.

Early that evening, he strolled out onto the balcony. Some friends joined him there. Suddenly, from the shadows, someone fired a single rifle blast. A bullet smashed into Dr. King's neck. The bullet's force was so great that it ripped the necktie right off him. Within an hour, Dr. King was dead. The death of this great African-American leader shocked the nation. Police quickly began a massive search for the assassin.

Grouped around Dr. Martin Luther King's body, his friends point to the source of the rifle shot that felled him. But the assassin had already fled.

2   The police figured out that the fatal shot had come from a nearby rooming house. The assassin had been sloppy. He had left his rifle near the scene. The police were able to get a clear fingerprint off this weapon. They traced the print to a small-time crook named James Earl Ray.

3   James Earl Ray? Just the thought of Ray as an assassin baffled the police. What reason did he have to shoot Dr. King? He was not a known racist or King hater. In fact, James Earl Ray had never seemed like much of a threat to anyone. He had dropped out of high school after 10th grade. He had tried army life, but with no success. Eventually, he had turned to a life of crime.

4   But Ray had not been very good at that, either. He once dropped his wallet during a robbery. That made it easy for police to prove he was the thief. Another time he was caught after falling out of a getaway car. His only "success" came in 1967. That year, he broke out of the Missouri State Prison. Even then, police were not exactly terrified. They put a puny $50 reward out for his capture.

5   And yet, *his* fingerprint was on the gun that killed Dr. King. So the police went looking for Ray. This time they set the reward at $100,000. But for the first time ever, they had trouble catching him. The man who had botched most of his other crimes now acted like a real, professional criminal.

6   First he fled to Toronto. There he obtained a Canadian passport. In those days that was easy to do. Ray simply paid $8 and swore that he was a Canadian citizen. The name he used was Ramon Sneyd.

7   Ray stayed in Canada for about a month. Then, on May 5, he used his phony passport to fly to England. He arrived in London on May 6. Soon after that, he flew to Portugal for five days. The reason for these trips has never been clear. Some people think Ray was just trying to elude police. Others think he was meeting someone who paid him to assassinate Dr. King. No one knows for sure.

8   Meanwhile, U.S. agents had picked up Ray's trail. They, too, knew how easy it was to get a Canadian passport. So they asked the police in Canada to sift through some 300,000 passport

applications. At last, one officer found Ray's photo on a form for Ramon Sneyd. Suddenly the manhunt heated up.

9   Back in England, Ray bounced from one cheap hotel to another. He must have known that the police were closing in. Using the name Sneyd, he called several newspapers. He asked how he could join some white army group in Africa. Ray must have thought he would be safe there. "Foreign legions" were famous for not asking about a person's history. One newspaper reporter suggested that Ray go to Belgium. Some white army groups were recruiting new soldiers there.

10   By now, however, the net had closed in on Ray. On June 8, "Sneyd" went to the airport. Just as he was about to board his plane to Belgium, the English police arrested him. They sent Ray back to the United States. He pleaded guilty and received a sentence of 99 years in prison. The day after he was sentenced, Ray changed his story. He tried to take back his plea, claiming that he had been forced to plead guilty. But it was too late. No one was listening.

11   For many people, the sentencing of James Earl Ray ended the story. But for others, questions remain. The most important one is this: Did Ray act alone? Agents for the U.S. government have always maintained that he did. But other people disagree. In 1978 a special panel studied the case. Panel members found a "likelihood" that other people were involved. James Earl Ray's own father said, "[James] couldn't have planned it alone. He wasn't smart enough for that."

12   If Ray did not act alone, then who helped him? Who told him what to do? Who planned—and paid for—his escape? No one knows. Some believe that a group of racists masterminded the killing. Others think U.S. leaders were behind the plot. According to this theory, the leaders did not like Dr. King. They did not like the way he stirred up the African-American community.

13   If Ray did take directions from someone, why did he do it? What could have persuaded him to kill Dr. King? Many think his motive was simple. He wanted money. All the other crimes he had committed had been for money. According to one rumor, Ray was paid $50,000 for the murder. But like the other theories, this one has never been proven.

14   Many years have now passed since the assassination. James Earl Ray died in prison on April 23, 1998. The whole may never be known. But one fact remains. No one else has been charged in the murder of Dr. King. James Earl Ray is still the only one who ever served time for the assassination.

A | Finding the Main Idea

One statement below expresses the main idea of the article. One statement is too general, or too broad. The other statement explains only part of the article; it is too narrow. Label the statements using the following key:

M—Main Idea   **B—Too Broad**   **N—Too Narrow**

_____ 1. Details about the assassination of Martin Luther King, Jr., by James Earl Ray remain a mystery.

_____ 2. Certain crimes fascinate and puzzle people long after the court decision has been made.

_____ 3. James Earl Ray was able to get a Canadian passport just by swearing that he was a Canadian citizen.

_____ Score 15 points for a correct M answer.

_____ Score 5 points for each correct B or N answer.

_____ **Total Score:** Finding the Main Idea

B | Recalling Facts

How well do you remember the facts in the article? Put an X in the box next to the answer that correctly completes each statement about the article.

1. Dr. King was killed by a blast from a
   ☐ a. rifle.
   ☐ b. handgun.
   ☐ c. machine gun.

2. James Earl Ray's education had ended after
   ☐ a. the eighth grade.
   ☐ b. one year of college.
   ☐ c. the 10th grade.

3. Police went after James Earl Ray because
   ☐ a. they knew he was a racist and a King hater.
   ☐ b. his fingerprints were on the weapon they had found.
   ☐ c. he looked guilty and ran away.

4. Ray first fled to Canada, then to
   ☐ a. England.
   ☐ b. France.
   ☐ c. Portugal.

5. English police arrested Ray just as he was about to
   ☐ a. assassinate the prime minister of England.
   ☐ b. go back into his hotel in London.
   ☐ c. board a plane for Belgium.

Score 5 points for each correct answer.

_____ **Total Score:** Recalling Facts

C | Making Inferences

When you combine your own experience and information from a text to draw a conclusion that is not directly stated in that text, you are making an inference. Below are five statements that may or may not be inferences based on information in the article. Label the statements using the following key:

C—Correct Inference　　　　**F—Faulty Inference**

_____ 1. Police were not very interested in finding the assassin of Martin Luther King, Jr.

_____ 2. The police had probably kept their eyes on James Earl Ray even before the assassination because they expected him to try to kill Dr. King.

_____ 3. U.S. agents felt that they could count on help from the Canadian police.

_____ 4. James Earl Ray felt safe and comfortable during his stay in England.

_____ 5. To get a Canadian passport in 1968, you needed a photograph of yourself.

Score 5 points for each correct answer.

_____ **Total Score:** Making Inferences

D | Using Words Precisely

Each numbered sentence below contains an underlined word or phrase from the article. Following the sentence are three definitions. One definition is closest to the meaning of the underlined word. One definition is opposite or nearly opposite. Label those two definitions using the following key; do not label the remaining definition.

C—Closest　　　　**O—Opposite or Nearly Opposite**

1. They put a <u>puny</u> $50 reward out for his capture.

_____ a. generous

_____ b. very small

_____ c. puzzling

2. The man who had <u>botched</u> most of his other crimes now acted like a real, professional criminal.

_____ a. ruined

_____ b. planned

_____ c. successfully performed

3. "<u>Foreign</u> legions" were famous for not asking about a person's history.

_____ a. having to do with laws

_____ b. having to do with your own country

_____ c. having to do with another country

4. Some people think that Ray was just trying to <u>elude</u> police.

_____ a. dodge

_____ b. seek out

_____ c. help

5. Agents for the U.S. government have always <u>maintained</u> that he did.

_____ a. recalled

_____ b. declared to be true

_____ c. denied

_____ Score 3 points for each correct C answer.

_____ Score 2 points for each correct O answer.

_____ **Total Score:** Using Words Precisely

Enter the four total scores in the spaces below, and add them together to find your Reading Comprehension Score. Then record your score on the graph on page 103.

Score	Question Type	Lesson 10
_____	Finding the Main Idea	
_____	Recalling Facts	
_____	Making Inferences	
_____	Using Words Precisely	
_____	**Reading Comprehension Score**	

Author's Approach

Put an X in the box next to the correct answer.

1. The authors use the first sentence of the article to

☐ a. inform the reader about Dr. King's assassination.

☐ b. describe the qualities of Dr. King.

☐ c. compare Dr. King and his friends.

2. The main purpose of the first paragraph is to

☐ a. prove that James Earl Ray assassinated Dr. King.

☐ b. show how quickly the search for Dr. King's killer began.

☐ c. present details about Dr. King's assassination.

3. Which of the following statements from the article best describes James Earl Ray after the assassination?

☐ a. In fact, James Earl Ray had never seemed like much of a threat to anyone.

☐ b. The man who had botched most of his other crimes now acted like a real, professional criminal.

☐ c. Another time he was caught after falling out of a getaway car.

4. Judging by statements from the article "Assassin!" you can conclude that the authors want the reader to think that

☐ a. everyone agrees that James Earl Ray acted alone when he killed Dr. King.

☐ b. many people suspect that James Earl Ray was taking orders from someone else when he shot Dr. King.

☐ c. James Earl Ray didn't really kill Dr. King.

_____ Number of correct answers

Record your personal assessment of your work on the Critical Thinking Chart on page 104.

Summarizing and Paraphrasing

Follow the directions provided for questions 1 and 2. Put an X in the box next to the correct answer for question 3.

1. Look for the important ideas and events in paragraphs 4 and 5. Summarize those paragraphs in one or two sentences.

_____

_____

_____

2. Complete the following one-sentence summary of the article using the lettered phrases from the phrase bank below. Write the letters on the lines.

Phrase Bank

a. how police hunted down and captured James Earl Ray and how courts convicted and sentenced him

b. theories about whether James Earl Ray worked with others in the assassination of Dr. King.

c. the assassination of Dr. King

The article "Assassin!" begins with _____, goes on to

explain _____, and ends with _____.

3. Read the statement from the article below. Then read the paraphrase of that statement. Choose the reason that best tells why the paraphrase does not say the same thing as the statement.

Statement: To get a Canadian passport, all Ray had to do was pay $8 and swear that he was a Canadian citizen.

Paraphrase: Ray was given a Canadian passport after he swore that he was a Canadian citizen.

☐ a. Paraphrase says too much.

☐ b. Paraphrase doesn't say enough.

☐ c. Paraphrase doesn't agree with the statement about the article.

_____ Number of correct answers

Record your personal assessment of your work on the Critical Thinking Chart on page 104.

Critical Thinking

Put an X in the box next to the correct answer for questions 1 and 2. Follow the directions provided for the other questions.

1. Which of the following statements from the article is an opinion rather than a fact?

☐ a. James Earl Ray is still the only one who has ever served time for the assassination.

☐ b. "[James] couldn't have planned it alone. He wasn't smart enough for that."

☐ c. Ray stayed in Canada for about a month.

2. Judging by the events in the article, you can predict that the following might happen next:

☐ a. People who paid Ray to kill Dr. King will soon start feeling sorry for their part in the crime and will confess to police.

☐ b. The real killer will soon confess and Ray will be found innocent.

☐ c. Ray will remain solely responsible for King's death.

3. Choose from the letters below to correctly complete the following statement. Write the letters on the lines.

In the article, _____ and _____ are different.

a. the way Ray acted after the assassination

b. the way Ray acted before the assassination

c. the way a professional criminal might act

4. Read paragraph 2. Then choose from the letters below to correctly complete the following statement. Write the letters on the lines.

According to paragraph 2, _____ because _____.

a. James Earl Ray was not a known racist

b. police immediately connected James Earl Ray to the assassination

c. police found James Earl Ray's fingerprint on the rifle

5. Which paragraphs from the article provide evidence that supports your answer to question 3?

_____

_____ Number of correct answers

Record your personal assessment of your work on the Critical Thinking Chart on page 104.

Personal Response

If you could ask the author of the article one question, what would it be?

_____

_____

_____

_____

Self-Assessment

Before reading this article, I already knew _____

_____

_____

_____

_____

Compare and Contrast

Think about the articles you have read in Unit Two. Pick the three articles that taught you the most facts. Write the titles of the articles in the first column of the chart below. Use information you learned from the articles to fill in the empy boxes in the chart.

Title	Which facts in the article were new to you?	Which facts in the article did you already know?	What historical period did this article tell about?

The article I learned the most from was _____. I was most surprised when I read about

_____

_____

Words-per-Minute Table

Unit Two

Directions: If you were timed while reading an article, refer to the Reading Time you recorded in the box at the end of the article. Use this words-per-minute table to determine your reading speed for that article. Then plot your reading speed on the graph on page 102.

Lesson / No. of Words	6 / 1,097	7 / 1,090	8 / 1,138	9 / 1,134	10 / 935	Seconds
1:30	731	727	759	756	623	90
1:40	658	654	683	680	561	100
1:50	598	595	621	619	510	110
2:00	549	545	569	567	468	120
2:10	506	503	525	523	432	130
2:20	470	467	488	486	401	140
2:30	439	436	455	454	374	150
2:40	411	409	427	425	351	160
2:50	387	385	402	400	330	170
3:00	366	363	379	378	312	180
3:10	346	344	359	358	295	190
3:20	329	327	341	340	281	200
3:30	313	311	325	324	267	210
3:40	299	297	310	309	255	220
3:50	286	284	297	296	244	230
4:00	274	273	285	284	234	240
4:10	263	262	273	272	224	250
4:20	253	252	263	262	216	260
4:30	244	242	253	252	208	270
4:40	235	234	244	243	200	280
4:50	227	226	235	235	193	290
5:00	219	218	228	227	187	300
5:10	212	211	220	219	181	310
5:20	206	204	213	213	175	320
5:30	199	198	207	756	170	330
5:40	194	192	201	200	165	340
5:50	188	187	195	194	160	350
6:00	183	182	190	189	156	360
6:10	178	177	185	184	152	370
6:20	173	172	180	680	148	380
6:30	169	168	175	174	144	390
6:40	165	164	171	170	140	400
6:50	161	160	167	166	137	410
7:00	157	156	163	162	134	420
7:10	153	152	159	158	130	430
7:20	150	149	155	155	128	440
7:30	146	145	152	151	125	450
7:40	143	142	148	148	122	460
7:50	140	139	145	145	119	470
8:00	137	136	142	142	117	480

Minutes and Seconds

Plotting Your Progress: Reading Speed

Unit Two

Directions: If you were timed while reading an article, write your words-per-minute rate for that article in the box under the number of the lesson. Then plot your reading speed on the graph by putting a small X on the line directly above the number of the lesson, across from the number of words per minute you read. As you mark your speed for each lesson, graph your progress by drawing a line to connect the X's.

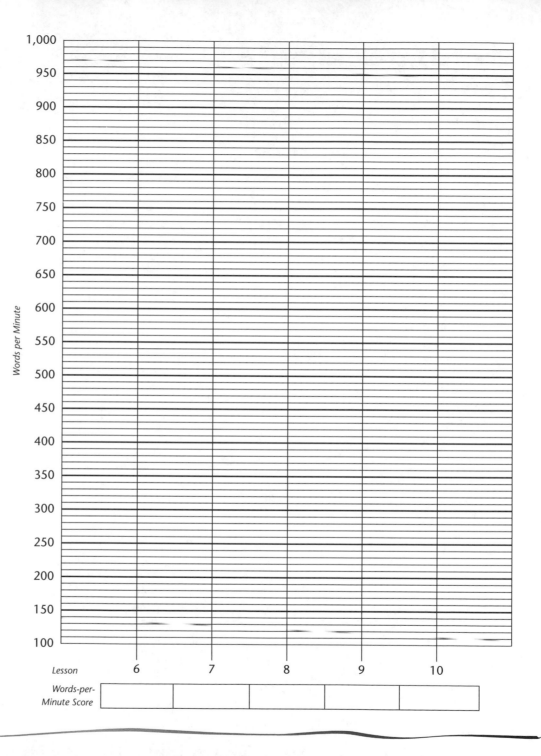

Lesson	6	7	8	9	10
Words-per-Minute Score					

Plotting Your Progress: Reading Comprehension

Unit Two

Directions: Write your Reading Comprehension Score for each lesson in the box under the number of the lesson. Then plot your score on the graph by putting a small X on the line directly above the number of the lesson and across from the score you earned. As you mark your score for each lesson, graph your progress by drawing a line to connect the X's.

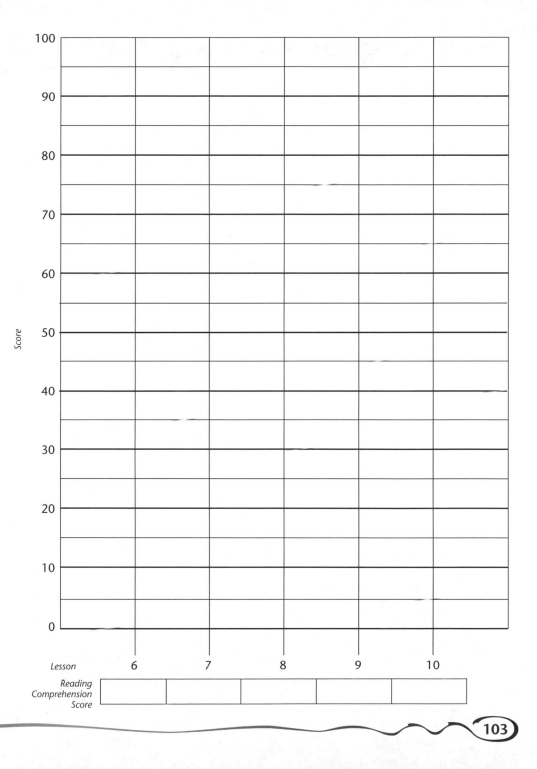

Plotting Your Progress: Critical Thinking

Unit Two

Directions: Work with your teacher to evaluate your responses to the Critical Thinking questions for each lesson. Then fill in the appropriate spaces in the chart below. For each lesson and each type of Critical Thinking question, do the following: Mark a minus sign (–) in the box to indicate areas in which you feel you could improve. Mark a plus sign (+) to indicate areas in which you feel you did well. Mark a minus-slash-plus sign (–/+) to indicate areas in which you had mixed success. Then write any comments you have about your performance, including ideas for improvement.

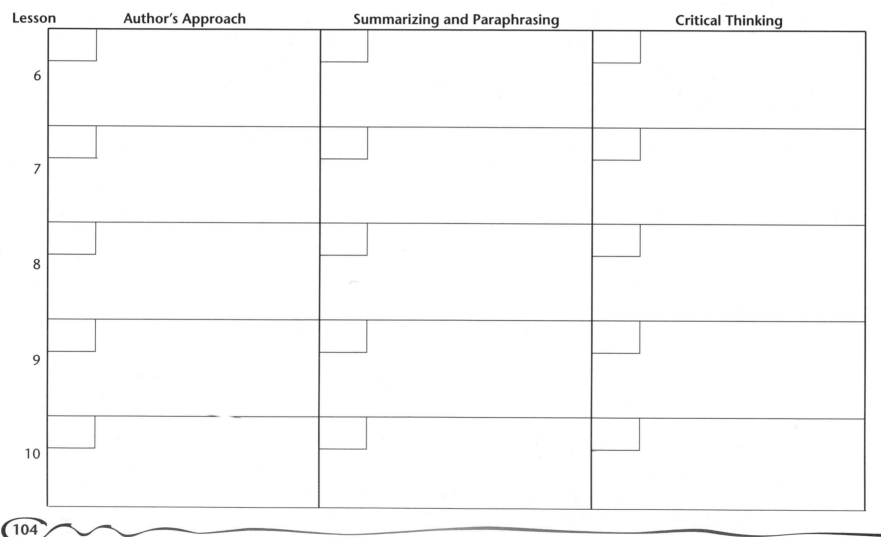

Lesson	Author's Approach	Summarizing and Paraphrasing	Critical Thinking
6			
7			
8			
9			
10			

UNIT THREE

Machine Gun Kelly

The police called him Public Enemy Number One. His wife, Kathryn, nicknamed him "Machine Gun" Kelly. To be sure, George R. Kelly was a criminal. There is no doubt about that. And he certainly talked like a real tough guy. Kelly liked to brag that "no copper [police officer] will ever take me alive." But was he all that bad? Was he the terror that the press made him out to be? Or was Kelly just an easygoing thief who happened to marry the wrong woman?

George Kelly, an easygoing petty thief, got into real trouble when he kidnapped a rich oilman. Both "Machine Gun" Kelly and his wife, Kathryn, were given life sentences for the crime Kathryn masterminded.

2   Kelly began his life of crime as a bootlegger during the 1920s. (A bootlegger is someone who sells illegal liquor.) But he wasn't very good at it.

    The police usually caught him. They either kicked him out of town or gave him a few months in jail. As one person put it, Kelly was "a good-natured slob, a bootlegger who spilled more [liquor] than he delivered."

3   That changed in 1927, the year Kelly met Kathryn Shannon. Before their fateful meeting, Kelly didn't even like guns. And he never hurt anyone. But Kathryn was an ambitious and ruthless woman. She soon saw that despite all the tough talk, George Kelly was really just a marshmallow. "You've got to be able to hurt people," she told him. "You've got to be tough or nobody will respect you."

4   Kathryn and Kelly were married, and she set out to toughen him up. She gave him a machine gun. She made him practice shooting walnuts off fence posts. In time, he became good enough to write his name on a wall with bullets. Kathryn also made sure that Kelly's reputation grew. She dreamed up phony stories about the big banks Kelly robbed. Kathryn even gave away empty bullet shells saying, "Have a souvenir of my husband, Machine Gun Kelly."

5   By 1931 Kelly had moved up the criminal ladder. The former bootlegger began to rob real banks. But he picked small country banks without much money. That was not good enough for Kathryn. She wanted to do something big. She had read stories about kidnappers getting huge ransoms. She began nagging Kelly to kidnap someone with lots of money. It was the only way to get rich, she insisted.

6   "Too risky," Kelly told her. But she kept pushing. Finally—as usual—Machine Gun Kelly gave in. He joined up with Albert Bates, another petty crook. They agreed to kidnap a rich Oklahoma City oilman named Charles Urschel.

7   On the night of July 22, 1933, Kelly and Bates broke into Urschel's home. They found the oilman and his wife playing cards with another couple. That confused Kelly. He was so incompetent that he hadn't bothered to find out what Urschel looked like. "Which one's Urschel?" he barked.

8   Neither man answered. "All right," Kelly said at last, "we'll take both of you."

9   Kelly and Bates drove off with the two men. After a while, Kelly thought to look in their wallets. Only then did he discover who the real Urschel was. He and Bates kicked the other man out of the car, then continued on with the blindfolded Urschel.

10   They took the oilman to a ranch owned by Kathryn's parents in Paradise, Texas. From there, the Kellys demanded a ransom of $200,000. The Urschel family agreed to pay. But with Machine Gun Kelly in charge, collecting the money wasn't easy. Kelly missed one meeting because he couldn't get his car started. Finally, after eight days, he collected the ransom.

11   Kathryn now wanted to kill Urschel. For once in his life, Kelly stood up to her. He convinced Bates and Kathryn to let Urschel go. Kelly pointed out that shooting him would "be bad for future business."

12   All this time, Charles Urschel had been alert and listening. The oilman had a keen memory. He noticed many

details about his kidnapping. He hoped the police could later use these details to catch his captors. Urschel noted that the car ride had taken about 12 hours over bumpy roads. He also noticed that a plane passed overhead twice a day. He even figured out the times—9:15 A.M. and 5:45 P.M.

13   After his release, Urschel gave these facts to agents from the Federal Bureau of Investigation (FBI). They knew what the 12-hour ride over bumpy roads meant. It meant the ranch was within 300 miles of Oklahoma City. The agents also studied hundreds of flight plans. They found the spot where daily flights crossed at 9:15 A.M. and 5:45 P.M. That spot was Paradise.

14   The FBI was now hot on the trail of Machine Gun Kelly. Agents labeled him Public Enemy Number One. Kelly and his wife ran, but they couldn't

hide. Investigators tracked them down at a cheap hotel in Memphis, Tennessee. Three police officers burst into Kelly's room. One shoved a shotgun into Kelly's stomach. Poor old Machine Gun gave up without a fight. "I've been waiting for you all night," he said softly.

15   At their trial, Kathryn turned against her husband. She tried to put all the blame on him. No one listened. Machine Gun, Kathryn, and Bates all got life sentences. It was a pitiful end for this so-called tough guy. Prison life at Leavenworth and Alcatraz was hard on George Machine Gun Kelly. His fellow inmates often laughed at him. They even gave him a new nickname— "Pop Gun" Kelly.

16   Just before he died in 1954, Kelly wrote a letter to his former victim, Charles Urschel. "These five words

seem written in fire on the walls of my cell," Kelly wrote. *"Nothing can be worth this!"* He might have said the same thing about his marriage to Kathryn.

If you have been timed while reading this article, enter your reading time below. Then turn to the Words-per-Minute Table on page 147 and look up your reading speed (words per minute). Enter your reading speed on the graph on page 148.

Reading Time: Lesson 11

_____ : _____
Minutes   Seconds

A **Finding the Main Idea**

One statement below expresses the main idea of the article. One statement is too general, or too broad. The other statement explains only part of the article; it is too narrow. Label the statements using the following key:

M—Main Idea　　**B—Too Broad**　　**N—Too Narrow**

_____ 1. The FBI considered Machine Gun Kelly a dangerous criminal.

_____ 2. When Machine Gun Kelly broke into Charles Urschel's house to kidnap him, he couldn't recognize Urschel.

_____ 3. Machine Gun Kelly, encouraged by his wife, Kathryn, became a famous robber and kidnapper during the 1930s.

_____ Score 15 points for a correct M answer.

_____ Score 5 points for each correct B or N answer.

_____ **Total Score:** Finding the Main Idea

 B **Recalling Facts**

How well do you remember the facts in the article? Put an X in the box next to the answer that correctly completes each statement about the article.

1. George Kelly began his life of crime as a

☐ a. train robber.

☐ b. petty thief.

☐ c. bootlegger.

2. To help George improve his machine gun skills, Kathryn made him practice shooting

☐ a. tin cans thrown into the air.

☐ b. walnuts off fence posts.

☐ c. a target with a big bull's-eye in the center.

3. To get rich, Kathryn urged George to

☐ a. rob a big bank in a major city.

☐ b. threaten to blow up a government building if they weren't given a million dollars.

☐ c. kidnap a rich person and demand a huge ransom.

4. After the $200,000 was paid, Kathryn wanted to

☐ a. kill Mr. Urschel.

☐ b. let Mr. Urschel go immediately.

☐ c. make Mr. Urschel part of the gang.

5. Machine Gun and Kathryn were captured in

☐ a. Memphis, Tennessee.

☐ b. Nashville, Tennessee.

☐ c. Tallahassee, Florida.

Score 5 points for each correct answer.

_____ **Total Score:** Recalling Facts

C | Making Inferences

When you combine your own experience and information from a text to draw a conclusion that is not directly stated in that text, you are making an inference. Below are five statements that may or may not be inferences based on information in the article. Label the statements using the following key:

C—Correct Inference   F—Faulty Inference

_____ 1. Machine Gun Kelly would probably never have committed any crimes if he hadn't met Kathryn.

_____ 2. The crime of bootlegging was considered less serious than the crime of kidnapping.

_____ 3. Country banks didn't hold as much money as city banks because most country people were poorer than most city people.

_____ 4. Machine Gun Kelly always planned his crimes carefully, with great attention to every detail.

_____ 5. Although Machine Gun Kelly was willing to commit many crimes, he did not wish to commit murder.

Score 5 points for each correct answer.

_____ **Total Score:** Making Inferences

D | Using Words Precisely

Each numbered sentence below contains an underlined word or phrase from the article. Following the sentence are three definitions. One definition is closest to the meaning of the underlined word. One definition is opposite or nearly opposite. Label those two definitions using the following key; do not label the remaining definition.

C—Closest   O—Opposite or Nearly Opposite

1. But Kathryn was an <u>ambitious</u> and ruthless woman.

_____ a. popular

_____ b. full of the drive to succeed

_____ c. lazy

2. He hoped the police could later use these details to catch his <u>captors</u>.

_____ a. people who capture others

_____ b. people who set others free

_____ c. people who kill others

3. He joined up with Albert Bates, another <u>petty</u> crook.

_____ a. major

_____ b. cute

_____ c. unimportant

4. He was so <u>incompetent</u> that he hadn't bothered to find out what Urschel looked like.

_____ a. lacking ability

_____ b. capable

_____ c. surprised

5. The oilman had a <u>keen</u> memory.

_____ a. dull

_____ b. happy

_____ c. sharp

_____ Score 3 points for each correct C answer.

_____ Score 2 points for each correct O answer.

_____ **Total Score:** Using Words Precisely

Enter the four total scores in the spaces below, and add them together to find your Reading Comprehension Score. Then record your score on the graph on page 149.

Score	Question Type	Lesson 11
_____	Finding the Main Idea	
_____	Recalling Facts	
_____	Making Inferences	
_____	Using Words Precisely	
_____	**Reading Comprehension Score**	

Author's Approach

Put an X in the box next to the correct answer.

1. The main purpose of the first paragraph is to

☐ a. describe Kathryn Kelly.

☐ b. inform the reader about the crimes that Machine Gun Kelly committed.

☐ c. raise doubts about whether Machine Gun Kelly was really dangerous.

2. What is the authors' purpose in writing "Machine Gun Kelly"?

☐ a. to express an opinion about kidnappers

☐ b. to describe a situation in which one person was greatly influenced by another person

☐ c. to emphasize the similarities between Machine Gun Kelly and Kathryn Kelly

3. How is the authors' purpose for writing the article expressed in paragraph 3?

☐ a. The authors state that Kelly met Kathryn Shannon in 1927.

☐ b. The authors suggest that Kathryn was the reason why Kelly began to commit more serious crimes.

☐ c. The authors explain that Kelly didn't hurt anyone in his early crimes.

4. The author tells this story mainly by

☐ a. describing events in the order they happened.

☐ b. comparing different topics.

☐ c. using their imagination and creativity.

_____ Number of correct answers

Record your personal assessment of your work on the Critical Thinking Chart on page 150.

Summarizing and Paraphrasing

Put an X in the box next to the correct answer for questions 1 and 3. Follow the directions provided for question 2.

1. Below are summaries of the article. Choose the summary that says all the most important things about the article but in the fewest words.

   ☐ a. The kidnapping of a rich oilman named Charles Urschel was the final crime in the life of Machine Gun Kelly.

   ☐ b. Encouraged in his life of crime by his wife, Kathryn, Machine Gun Kelly committed a series of crimes in the 1920s and 1930s. He and his wife were finally arrested and put in prison after kidnapping a rich oilman.

   ☐ c. Machine Gun Kelly started his life of crime as a bootlegger and then began to commit more serious crimes. His wife gave him the nickname Machine Gun and encouraged him to practice using that kind of gun in his crimes.

2. Reread paragraph 11 in the article. Below, write a summary of the paragraph in no more than 25 words.

   _____

   _____

   _____

   _____

   Reread your summary and decide whether it covers the important ideas in the paragraph. Next, decide how to shorten the summary to 15 words or less without leaving out any essential information. Write this summary below.

   _____

   _____

   _____

3. Choose the sentence that correctly restates the following sentence from the article: "[Kathryn] soon saw that despite all the tough talk, George Kelly was really just a marshmallow."

   ☐ a. Kathryn believed that she was tough and George Kelly was weak.

   ☐ b. When George Kelly talked tough, Kathryn thought that he looked like a marshmallow.

   ☐ c. Kathryn discovered that even though George Kelly acted tough, he wasn't especially violent or mean.

   _____ Number of correct answers

   Record your personal assessment of your work on the Critical Thinking Chart on page 150.

Critical Thinking

Follow the directions provided for questions 1, 2, and 3. Put an X in the box next to the correct answer question 4.

1. For each statement below, write *O* if it expresses an opinion or write *F* if it expresses a fact.

   _____ a. Some people in prison gave George Kelly a new nickname—"Pop Gun" Kelly.

   _____ b. The Kellys demanded a ransom of $200,000 for the release of Charles Urschel.

   _____ c. Kathryn Kelly was a good wife for George Kelly.

2. Using what you know about Machine Gun Kelly and what is told about Kathryn Kelly in the article, name three ways Machine Gun is similar to Kathryn and three ways Machine Gun is different from her. Cite the paragraph number(s) where you found details in the article to support your conclusions.

Similarities

_____

_____

_____

Differences

_____

_____

_____

3. Think about cause-effect relationships in the article. Fill in the blanks in the chart, drawing from the letters below.

Cause	Effect
Kathryn wanted more money.	_____
Urschel reported the times when he heard airplanes.	_____
_____	The ransom money wasn't exchanged on time.

a. FBI agents checked on flight schedules.

b. Kathryn urged Machine Gun to kidnap Urschel.

c. Machine Gun couldn't start his car one day.

4. What did you have to do to answer question 2?

☐ a. find an opinion (what someone thinks about something)

☐ b. find a description (how something looks)

☐ c. find a comparison (how things are the same)

_____ Number of correct answers

Record your personal assessment of your work on the Critical Thinking Chart on page 150.

Personal Response

What do you think was Machine Gun Kelly's biggest mistake?

_____

_____

_____

Self-Assessment

Before reading the article, I already knew _____

_____

_____

_____

The Man with Many Faces

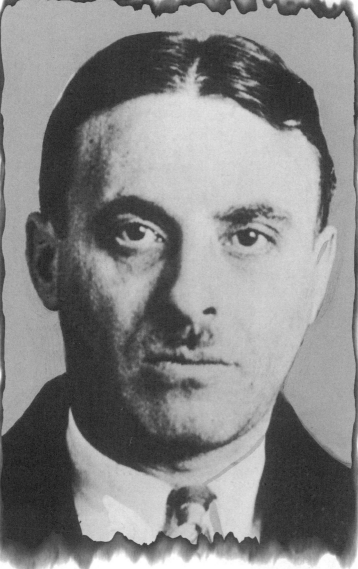

His parents named him Stephen Jacob Weinberg, but he rarely used that name. Weinberg, who was born in Brooklyn in 1890, loved to make up new names for himself. He loved to pretend he was someone with an important job. Often he used the name Stanley Clifford Weyman or something close to it. For nearly forty years, Weinberg played all sorts of make-believe roles. This daring

This man could be a Serbian army officer, a Romanian diplomat, a U.S. Army pilot, a doctor, or a prison reform expert. Talented impostor Stephen Jacob Weinberg could convince people that he could be and do almost anything.

impostor fooled most people. But sooner or later, someone always found out who he really was. Sometimes the police let him off with a warning. Other times he went to jail.

2 Weinberg was a bright young man. With some hard work, he might have become a doctor or a pilot or a diplomat or a navy officer. But Weinberg had two problems. First, he lacked the patience to go to college and study for any of these professions. Second, he wanted to hold all these jobs. He decided there was only one thing to do. He would pretend to be whatever he wanted. That way he could be a doctor one day and something else the next.

3 Being a good impostor isn't easy. Weinberg quickly learned how hard it could be. In 1912 he posed as "Clifford Weinberg, the American Consul to Morocco." Earlier, Weinberg had stolen a camera from a photographer's shop. One day the shop owner showed up at a photo session for "consul" Weinberg. The owner recognized the "consul" as a thief, and Weinberg ended up in jail.

4 After he got out, Weinberg tried to get honest work. But every job he got seemed dull next to the jobs he dreamed up in his head. So Weinberg went back to his fantasies. He became "Lieutenant Royale St. Cyr," a U.S. Army pilot. He also took on the role of a U.S. Navy officer. For a while, he posed as an army officer from Serbia. He also became "Ethan Allen Weinberg," a diplomat from Romania. Some people said Weinberg looked good in a military uniform. He must have—he certainly wore enough of them! He also wore plenty of prison uniforms. Between 1913 and 1918, he was in and out of jail at least four times.

5 By 1920 Weinberg was ready for another challenge. A New York company needed a doctor to go to Peru. The doctor would check out health conditions at a work site there. A "Dr. Clifford Wyman" applied for the job. Like all the other applicants, he was interviewed by a real doctor. "Dr. Wyman" completely fooled the interviewer. He made such a good impression that he got the job.

6 Soon "Dr. Wyman" set sail for Peru. There he rented a fancy house, bought a nice car, and gave huge parties. He had all his bills sent to the company back in New York. The local workers liked "Dr. Wyman" very much. And why not? He simply approved everything they did. But at last, company officials found out who "Dr. Wyman" really was. They fired him but didn't press charges. Perhaps they were too embarrassed about hiring him in the first place!

7 In 1921 Princess Fatima of Afghanistan arrived in New York. She hoped to meet U.S. President Warren Harding. And she did. The meeting was set up by someone dressed as a naval officer. He said his name was "Sterling Clifford Wyman." No one questioned "Wyman." He seemed to know exactly what he was doing. He even got the princess to pay for all his expenses. (He told her it was an American custom.) She finally smartened up when "Wyman" offered to help her sell her priceless forty-two-carat diamond. Later, the police caught on as well. Weinberg was arrested and charged with impersonating a navy officer. He was sent to prison for two years.

8 Still, Weinberg refused to quit role-playing. He loved the thrill of it. A

little jail time seemed a small price to pay for such grand adventures. Once, Weinberg even tried to pass himself off as a "prison reform expert." There was just one problem. His old prison warden recognized him! Another time, Weinberg started up his own law office. But since he had no license to practice law, that led to another term behind bars.

9 During World War II, Weinberg began calling himself a "Selective Service consultant." That sounded pretty good. But what Weinberg was doing was illegal. He was teaching young men how to avoid serving in the army. He taught them, for example, how to fake deafness. Again, he was caught and sent to prison.

10 Weinberg got out of jail in 1948. He decided to become a reporter. As "Stanley Clifford Weyman," he got a job with the Erwin News Service. His task was to cover the United Nations. Mr. Erwin later said, "Weyman had good news sense—and he seemed to know everybody."

11 "Weyman" was so good, in fact, that he got his own radio show on WFDR.

Every day he gave a five-minute comment on the news. Once a week he had special guests join him on the show. They included top diplomats from all over the world. Some diplomats from Thailand were especially impressed with him. ("Weyman" had convinced them that he had worked as a spy on their behalf during World War II.) In 1951 the Thais offered "Weyman" a job as their own press officer. For Weinberg this was a dream come true. He would now be a real diplomat.

12 But, as usual, Weinberg was caught. He started wondering how the job would affect him as an American citizen. So he wrote a letter to the State Department asking about it. Officials there checked into Weinberg's background. It isn't hard to guess the rest of the story. The embarrassed Thais withdrew the job offer. And Weinberg lost his job with the Erwin News Service.

13 By 1960 Weinberg was an old man. He took a job working as a night clerk in a New York hotel. But he still had dreams of glory. One night two gunmen came in to rob the cash box.

Weinberg had no weapon, but he tried to fight off the robbers anyway. The gunmen shot him, then fled without the money. As Weinberg lay dying, perhaps he took some comfort in knowing his last role in life was that of a hero.

If you have been timed while reading this article, enter your reading time below. Then turn to the Words-per-Minute Table on page 147 and look up your reading speed (words per minute). Enter your reading speed on the graph on page 148.

Reading Time: Lesson 12

————— : —————
Minutes   Seconds

A | Finding the Main Idea

One statement below expresses the main idea of the article. One statement is too general, or too broad. The other statement explains only part of the article; it is too narrow. Label the statements using the following key:

M—Main Idea   B—Too Broad   N—Too Narrow

_____ 1. Impersonating other people may be illegal and can land a person in jail.

_____ 2. Stephen Jacob Weinberg was a daring impersonator who fooled people for years, even though it often landed him in prison.

_____ 3. Dressed as a naval officer, Stephen Jacob Weinberg fooled Princess Fatima into paying for his expenses in New York.

_____ Score 15 points for a correct M answer.

_____ Score 5 points for each correct B or N answer.

_____ **Total Score:** Finding the Main Idea

B | Recalling Facts

How well do you remember the facts in the article? Put an X in the box next to the answer that correctly completes each statement about the article.

1. A shop owner recognized Weinberg as the
   ☐ a. person who set fire to his store.
   ☐ b. thief who stole a camera from him.
   ☐ c. man who pretended to be a lawyer.

2. Posing as Dr. Wyman, Weinberg was sent to
   ☐ a. Peru.
   ☐ b. Serbia.
   ☐ c. Morocco.

3. Princess Fatima of Afghanistan hoped to meet
   ☐ a. the mayor of New York City.
   ☐ b. Stephen Jacob Weinberg.
   ☐ c. President Warren Harding.

4. Erwin News Service hired Weinberg to report on
   ☐ a. World War II.
   ☐ b. the United Nations.
   ☐ c. local news from New York City.

5. The State Department discovered that Weinberg had been offered the job of press officer in Thailand when he
   ☐ a. wrote them a letter.
   ☐ b. applied for a passport.
   ☐ c. announced it on the radio.

Score 5 points for each correct answer.

_____ **Total Score:** Recalling Facts

C | Making Inferences

When you combine your own experience and information from a text to draw a conclusion that is not directly stated in that text, you are making an inference. Below are five statements that may or may not be inferences based on information in the article. Label the statements using the following key:

C—Correct Inference   **F—Faulty Inference**

_____ 1. Many people are willing to believe what a stranger says, even when the stranger is lying.

_____ 2. No matter whom he was pretending to be, Weinberg seemed honest and self-confident.

_____ 3. A real doctor can always recognize another real doctor.

_____ 4. During World War II, men with certain physical disabilities were not required to serve in the army.

_____ 5. Time spent in prison always convinces criminals to change their ways.

Score 5 points for each correct answer.

_____ **Total Score:** Making Inferences

D | Using Words Precisely

Each numbered sentence below contains an underlined word or phrase from the article. Following the sentence are three definitions. One definition is closest to the meaning of the underlined word. One definition is opposite or nearly opposite. Label those two definitions using the following key. Do not label the remaining definition.

C—Closest   **O—Opposite or Nearly Opposite**

1. For a while, he <u>posed as</u> an army officer from Serbia.

_____ a. followed

_____ b. really became

_____ c. pretended to be

2. By 1920 Weinberg was ready for another <u>challenge</u>.

_____ a. easy task

_____ b. crime

_____ c. difficult task

3. He simply <u>approved</u> everything they did.

_____ a. accepted

_____ b. found fault with

_____ c. assigned

4. She finally smartened up when "Wyman" offered to help her sell her <u>priceless</u> forty-two-carat diamond.

_____ a. precious

_____ b. very old

_____ c. worthless

5. "Weyman" had <u>convinced</u> them that he had worked as a spy on their behalf during World War II.

_____ a. caused to doubt

_____ b. caused to believe

_____ c. blamed

_____ Score 3 points for each correct C answer.

_____ Score 2 points for each correct O answer.

_____ **Total Score:** Using Words Precisely

Enter the four total scores in the spaces below, and add them together to find your Reading Comprehension Score. Then record your score on the graph on page 149.

Score	Question Type	Lesson 12
_____	Finding the Main Idea	
_____	Recalling Facts	
_____	Making Inferences	
_____	Using Words Precisely	
_____	**Reading Comprehension Score**	

Author's Approach

Put an X in the box next to the correct answer.

1. From the statements below, choose the one that you believe the authors would agree with.

☐ a. Stephen Weinberg was a violent and dangerous criminal who should have been in prison.

☐ b. Stephen Weinberg's only crime was that he was a skillful liar, so he should never have been put in jail.

☐ c. Stephen Weinberg was an odd person who broke the law at times but was mostly harmless.

2. Choose the statement below that is the weakest argument for punishing, or even jailing, impostors.

☐ a. Some impostors harm others by pretending to have skills they don't have.

☐ b. The people the impostor fools feel silly when they learn the truth.

☐ c. Some impostors steal money while in disguise.

3. What do the authors imply by saying "'Dr. Wyman' completely fooled the interviewer. He made such a good impression that he got the job"?

☐ a. Stephen Weinberg was intelligent and good with words.

☐ b. The interviewer was not very smart.

☐ c. Stephen Weinberg was the only person who was interviewed for the job.

_____ Number of correct answers

Record your personal assessment of your work on the Critical Thinking Chart on page 150.

Summarizing and Paraphrasing

Follow the directions provided for question 1. Put an X in the box next to the correct answer for question 2.

1. Reread paragraph 3 in the article. Below, write a summary of the paragraph in no more than 25 words.

_____

_____

_____

Reread your summary and decide whether it covers the important ideas in the paragraph. Next, decide how to shorten the summary to 15 words or less without leaving out any essential information. Write this summary below.

_____

_____

_____

2. Read the statement about the article below. Then read the paraphrase of that statement. Choose the reason that best tells why the paraphrase does not say the same thing as the statement.

Statement: As a "Selective Service Consultant," Weinberg counseled young men about how they could avoid serving in the army.

Paraphrase: As a "Selective Service Consultant," Weinberg suggested faking deafness as a way to avoid serving in the army.

☐ a. Paraphrase says too much.

☐ b. Paraphrase doesn't say enough.

☐ c. Paraphrase doesn't agree with the statement about the article.

_____ Number of correct answers

Record your personal assessment of your work on the Critical Thinking Chart on page 150.

Critical Thinking

Put an X in the box next to the correct answer for questions 1, 2, and 4. Follow the directions provided for questions 3 and 5.

1. Which of the following statements from the article is an opinion rather than a fact?

☐ a. In 1921 Princess Fatima of Afghanistan arrived in New York.

☐ b. As Weinberg lay dying, perhaps he took some comfort in knowing that his last role in life was that of a hero.

☐ c. As 'Stanley Clifford Weyman,' he got a job with the Erwin News Service.

2. From the article, you can predict that if Stephen Weinberg were alive today, he would

☐ a. still be pretending to be someone he isn't.

☐ b. never get away with pretending to be someone he isn't.

☐ c. never even try to be an impostor because today it is too hard to fool anyone.

3. Choose from the letters below to correctly complete the following statement. Write the letters on the lines.

According to the article, _____ caused the State

Department to _____, and the effect was _____.

   a. Stephen Weinberg's letter to the State Department asking how the job of Thai press officer would affect him

   b. that the Thais withdrew the job offer

   c. tell the Thais that Stephen Weinberg had no credentials as a press officer

4. If you were looking for someone to fill a job, how could you use the information in the article to avoid choosing an impostor?

   ☐ a. You could avoid hiring the people who seem very eager to get the job.

   ☐ b. You could hire the person who seems most honest.

   ☐ c. You could check each applicant's background thoroughly.

5. In which paragraph did you find your information or details to answer question 3? _____

_____ Number of correct answers

Record your personal assessment of your work on the Critical Thinking Chart on page 150.

Personal Response

Why do you think Stephen Jacob Weinberg pretended to be someone else throughout his life?

_____

_____

_____

_____

Self-Assessment

A word or phrase in the article that I do not understand is _____

_____

_____

_____

_____

Was Lizzie Borden an Axe Murderer?

Lizzie Borden took
an axe
And gave her mother
forty whacks.
When she saw what she
had done,
She gave her father
forty-one.

This rhyme has been around for more than a hundred years. It describes Lizzie Borden as a cold-blooded killer. But is the rhyme accurate? Did Lizzie butcher her parents one hot August

Neighbors said that Lizzie Borden was kind and gentle. Yet when her father and stepmother were found murdered in their home, suspicion focused on Lizzie. She was the only one home at the time. Didn't she hear or see anything?

morning in 1892? Or did someone else commit the brutal murders?

2 The crimes took place in Fall River, Massachusetts. That's where thirty-two-year-old Lizzie Borden lived with her father, stepmother, and older sister, Emma. The morning of August 4, 1892, began quietly enough in the Borden house. Mr. Borden left for work around 9 A.M. Mrs. Borden started to do her housework. The maid, Bridget Sullivan, went outside to wash windows. Emma was away. She was visiting friends in a nearby town. And Lizzie? Well, Lizzie said she spent much of the morning out in the barn. She was getting things ready for a fishing trip she planned to take. The rest of the time, she said, she was in her room, lying down.

3 Sometime between 9 and 9:30 A.M., Mrs. Borden was making a bed in a second-floor bedroom. Someone crept into the room behind her. Without warning, the killer brought an axe down on Mrs. Borden's head. Nineteen times she was struck with the axe. Blood splattered all over the walls. By the time the killer was finished, Mrs. Borden lay dead. Her body was not found right away, however. When Mr. Borden came home around 10:30 A.M., he had no idea that anything was wrong.

4 Mr. Borden headed straight for the couch in the sitting room. He had not been feeling well, and the sweltering heat of the morning had drained his energy. He wanted to rest awhile. The maid was also feeling sick that day. A nap sounded like a good idea to her, too. Accordingly, Bridget Sullivan went up to her attic room and quickly fell asleep.

5 Once again the killer sprang into action. Before Mr. Borden knew what was happening, an axe struck him in the face. The killer delivered ten blows, leaving Mr. Borden—like his wife— dead in the house.

6 At 11:15 A.M. Lizzie Borden screamed to Bridget Sullivan. "Come down quick! Someone's killed Father!" With those words, Lizzie announced the horrible news. Soon neighbors, police officers, and reporters were swarming around the Borden home. One of the neighbors discovered Mrs. Borden's body in the upstairs bedroom. By evening, Lizzie's sister Emma had heard the news. She hurried home to be with Lizzie.

7 Meanwhile, questions swirled through the community. Who could have done such terrible deeds? And why? Suspicion centered on Lizzie. Her story didn't make sense. She said she had been out in the barn, but there were no footprints on the dusty barn floor. It looked to police as though no one had set foot in there for days or even weeks. In addition, the maid reported an interesting detail. When Mr. Borden came home that morning, Lizzie had stood at the top of the stairs, laughing in an odd way. And several hours after the murders, Lizzie was seen burning a piece of wood that looked like an axe handle.

8 Besides, many people whispered, no one else could have done it. The doors to the house were locked, so no intruder could have gotten in. Everyone knew that Lizzie hated her stepmother. And with Mr. and Mrs. Borden both dead, Lizzie and her sister would inherit half a million dollars.

9 Yet some questions could not be answered. There was blood all over the crime scenes. So how could it be that

no blood was found on Lizzie or her clothing? If Lizzie were the killer, where had she hidden the murder weapon? And how could she have stayed so calm during the hour between the two killings?

10   Some people decided that Lizzie's sister, Emma, was the murderer. She, too, hated her stepmother. In fact, Emma hated Mrs. Borden even more than Lizzie did. Lizzie was just a baby when her real mother died. But Emma was eleven years old. She was old enough to remember her mother—and to hate the woman who tried to replace her. Like Lizzie, Emma knew she would get a lot of money when her parents died. And although Emma had been staying with friends on the day of the murders, she could easily have sneaked back into town. She had a key to the house. She would have had no trouble unlocking the door.

11   Other people believed both sisters were innocent. After all, neither one had ever been violent before. They had always been kind and gentle. The Borden house had been broken into a few months earlier. Perhaps the thief had returned, this time with murder in mind. Or what about the enemies Mr. Borden had made in his business dealings? The killer could have been someone seeking revenge. A stranger could have slipped into the house while Lizzie was in the barn. During that time, the door was unlocked.

12   The police were in a difficult spot. The entire nation was watching the events in Fall River. Most police officers believed Lizzie was the killer. But they had no witness, no murder weapon, and no real evidence. It would be hard to make a case. Still, there was tremendous pressure on them to make an arrest. One week after the killings, they did. They arrested Lizzie Borden and charged her with two counts of murder.

13   The trial took place in June of 1893. It lasted thirteen days. Both sides did their best. But in the end, the jury simply could not believe that the calm, quiet Lizzie Borden had committed such awful acts. They spent one hour discussing the case. Then they found Lizzie not guilty.

14   In many ways, though, the jury's verdict did not matter. Lizzie's life was changed forever. Most people believed she was guilty. To this day, Lizzie Borden is not remembered for her love of animals. She is not remembered for the money she gave to the poor. She is remembered only as the woman who gave her mother "forty whacks" and then went on to give her father "forty-one."

If you have been timed while reading this article, enter your reading time below. Then turn to the Words-per-Minute Table on page 147 and look up your reading speed (words per minute). Enter your reading speed on the graph on page 148.

Reading Time: Lesson 13

_____ : _____
Minutes   *Seconds*

A | Finding the Main Idea

One statement below expresses the main idea of the article. One statement is too general, or too broad. The other statement explains only part of the article; it is too narrow. Label the statements using the following key:

M—Main Idea   **B—Too Broad**   **N—Too Narrow**

_____ 1. One of the most famous unsolved mysteries in Massachusetts is the murder of Lizzie Borden's parents in 1892.

_____ 2. To many people, Lizzie Borden seemed guilty of murdering her parents because her story about where she was when the crimes occurred didn't make sense.

_____ 3. Although Lizzie Borden was tried for the 1892 murder of her parents, there was never any solid evidence that she was guilty.

_____ Score 15 points for a correct M answer.

_____ Score 5 points for each correct B or N answer.

_____ **Total Score:** Finding the Main Idea

B | Recalling Facts

How well do you remember the facts in the article? Put an X in the box next to the answer that correctly completes each statement about the article.

1. The murders at the Borden home occurred
   ☐ a. on a hot August morning.
   ☐ b. during a hot August night.
   ☐ c. shortly after Mr. Borden remarried.

2. The murderer killed Mr. Borden
   ☐ a. when he discovered Mrs. Borden's body.
   ☐ b. during an argument.
   ☐ c. as he slept on the couch.

3. The maid reported that Lizzie had
   ☐ a. laughed strangely that morning.
   ☐ b. been out in the barn.
   ☐ c. lost her keys to the house.

4. People who blamed the Borden sisters for their parents' murders did not give this as a reason:
   ☐ a. A desire to inherit Mr. Borden's wealth.
   ☐ b. Revenge for driving away their boyfriends.
   ☐ c. Hatred for their stepmother.

5. At Lizzie's trial, the verdict was
   ☐ a. not guilty.
   ☐ b. not guilty, on grounds of insanity.
   ☐ c. thrown out because of prejudice on the part of the jury.

Score 5 points for each correct answer.

_____ **Total Score:** Recalling Facts

C Making Inferences

When you combine your own experience and information from a text to draw a conclusion that is not directly stated in that text, you are making an inference. Below are five statements that may or may not be inferences based on information in the article. Label the statements using the following key:

C—Correct Inference   **F—Faulty Inference**

_____ 1. Whoever killed Mr. and Mrs. Borden had to be strong and able to move quietly.

_____ 2. For a long time before the murders, there had been great unhappiness in the Borden household.

_____ 3. The members of the jury at Lizzie's trial were divided by the evidence and had to discuss several issues in depth before they came to an agreement.

_____ 4. An innocent person accused of a famous crime can be confident that once a jury finds him or her not guilty, the public will accept that verdict.

_____ 5. The public's desire to learn every detail of a well-known crime is nothing new.

Score 5 points for each correct answer.

_____ **Total Score:** Making Inferences

D Using Words Precisely

Each numbered sentence below contains an underlined word or phrase from the article. Following the sentence are three definitions. One definition is closest to the meaning of the underlined word. One definition is opposite or nearly opposite. Label those two definitions using the following key; do not label the remaining definition.

C—Closest   **O—Opposite or Nearly Opposite**

1. It describes Lizzie Borden as a cold-blooded killer.

_____ a. habitually late

_____ b. extremely tenderhearted and emotional

_____ c. without normal human feelings of pity and kindness

2. Or did someone else commit the brutal murders?

_____ a. extremely cruel

_____ b. local

_____ c. kind

3. Meanwhile, questions swirled through the community.

_____ a. moved in a straight line

_____ b. waited

_____ c. whirled

4. Suspicion centered on Lizzie.

_____ a. distrust

_____ b. faith

_____ c. excitement

5. The doors to the house were locked, so no <u>intruder</u> could have gotten in.

_____ a. one who belongs

_____ b. unwanted outsider

_____ c. instructor

_____ Score 3 points for each correct C answer.

_____ Score 2 points for each correct O answer.

_____ **Total Score:** Using Words Precisely

Enter the four total scores in the spaces below, and add them together to find your Reading Comprehension Score. Then record your score on the graph on page 149.

Score	Question Type	Lesson 13
_____	Finding the Main Idea	
_____	Recalling Facts	
_____	Making Inferences	
_____	Using Words Precisely	
_____	**Reading Comprehension Score**	

Author's Approach

Put an X in the box next to the correct answer.

1. Judging by statements from the article, you can conclude that the authors want the reader to think that

☐ a. Lizzie Borden killed her mother and her father.

☐ b. Lizzie Borden did not kill her mother and her father.

☐ c. we will never know for sure whether Lizzie Borden killed her mother and her father.

2. Choose the statement below that is the weakest argument for believing that Lizzie Borden was innocent of the crime.

☐ a. Lizzie looked too calm and quiet to commit murder.

☐ b. Lizzie was the only one at home at the time, besides the maid, and the doors were locked.

☐ c. There were no footprints on the dusty barn floor.

3. What do the authors imply by saying "Lizzie was just a baby when her real mother died"?

☐ a. Lizzie didn't remember her mother and probably didn't hate her stepmother for replacing her mother.

☐ b. Lizzie had never known a mother's love, and her lack of affection while growing up made her cold and heartless.

☐ c. Perhaps Lizzie's birth had something to do with her mother's death at such an early age.

4. The authors probably wrote this article to

☐ a. persuade readers that Lizzie Borden was innocent.

☐ b. inform readers about a fascinating mystery.

☐ c. show how easy it is to fool a jury if you act gentle.

_____ Number of correct answers

Record your personal assessment of your work on the Critical Thinking Chart on page 150.

Summarizing and Paraphrasing

Follow the directions provided for questions 1 and 2. Put an X in the box next to the correct answer for question 3.

1. Look for the important ideas and events in paragraphs 13 and 14. Summarize those paragraphs in one or two sentences.

_____

_____

_____

2. Complete the following one-sentence summary of the article using the lettered phrases from the phrase bank below. Write the letters on the lines.

Phrase Bank

a. the trial of Lizzie Borden and the jury's verdict

b. a description of the murders of Mr. and Mrs. Borden

c. theories about who the killer was

The article "Was Lizzie Borden an Axe Murderer?" begins with

_____, goes on to explain _____, and ends with

_____.

3. Choose the sentence that correctly restates the following sentence from the article: "A stranger *could* have slipped into the house while Lizzie was in the barn."

☐ a. A stranger must have entered the house while Lizzie was in the barn.

☐ b. The only time a stranger could have entered the house was when Lizzie was in the barn.

☐ c. It would have been possible for a stranger to enter the house when Lizzie was out in the barn.

_____ Number of correct answers

Record your personal assessment of your work on the Critical Thinking Chart on page 150.

Critical Thinking

Put an X in the box next to the correct answer for questions 1, 2, and 4. Follow the directions provided for the other questions.

1. Which of the following statements from the article is an opinion rather than a fact?

☐ a. The crimes took place in Fall River, Massachusetts.

☐ b. Her story didn't make sense.

☐ c. The Borden house had been broken into a few months earlier.

2. From the article, you can predict that if these murders happened today,

☐ a. no one would pay any attention to them.

☐ b. TV news reporters would be in the courtroom every day of the trial.

☐ c. the jury would find Lizzie Borden guilty.

3. Choose from the letters below to correctly complete the following statement. Write the letters on the lines.

On the positive side, _____, but on the negative side _____.

a. Lizzie and her sister became rich

b. many people were interested in the outcome of the trial

c. Lizzie's parents were murdered

4. What was one effect of the day's unbearable heat?

☐ a. Mr. Borden felt tired and decided to rest on the couch.

☐ b. Mr. Borden left for work at 9 o' clock in the morning.

☐ c. The maid decided to wash the windows.

5. In which paragraph did you find your information or details to answer question 4? _____

_____

_____ Number of correct answers

Record your personal assessment of your work on the Critical Thinking Chart on page 150.

Personal Response

I wonder why _____

_____

_____

_____

_____

Self-Assessment

From reading this article, I have learned _____

_____

_____

_____

_____

A Nazi War Criminal

Protected by a wall of bulletproof glass, former Nazi Adolf Eichmann listens to testimony of concentration camp survivors during his trial for the murder of 6 million people.

On the list of the world's worst criminals, Adolf Eichmann has to rank near the top. He was not just an ordinary criminal. He was a war criminal. Eichmann sent six million people to their deaths during World War II. Most frightening of all is that in his own warped mind, Eichmann thought he was doing the right thing.

2 Eichmann's road to evil began in 1932. That was when he joined the Nazi party. The Nazis were led by Adolf Hitler, a vile madman who wanted to take over Europe. Along the

way, Hitler hoped to wipe out all the Jews living there. Eichmann worked his way up in Germany's Nazi party. He rose to a position of great power. He became a specialist in what Hitler called the "Jewish problem." In other words, Eichmann was in charge of killing Jews.

3   Eichmann carried out his hateful work from 1938 to 1945. These were the years just before and during World War II. During this time, Germany controlled most of Europe. So millions of Jews from France to Poland came under Nazi rule. Eichmann began rounding them up and sending them to their deaths. "When I am finished with my work," he once bragged, "there will be no more Jews in Europe."

4   Eichmann shipped his victims to concentration camps. There, anyone who was not able to work was immediately killed. The old, the young, and the sick were sent directly to gas chambers. The rest were forced to work like slaves. A sign over the gate of one camp read, "Work Brings Freedom". That was a crucl hoax. The Nazis' real goal was to work Jews until

they couldn't work anymore. Then those Jews, too, were killed. By 1945 Adolf Eichmann and his henchmen had murdered six million Jews.

5   Hitler and the Nazis were finally defeated in 1945. As the war ended, Adolf Hitler killed himself. Other Nazi leaders were caught and put on trial for their war crimes. Most were hanged. But a few top Nazi leaders got away. One of them was Eichmann. In a strange twist of fate, Eichmann was captured at first. But no one knew who he was. He had disguised himself in a uniform stolen from a dead German soldier. He was put in a prisoner-of-war camp along with other low-ranking German soldiers. Before anyone figured out his true identity, he escaped.

6   The police from many countries searched for Eichmann. He was at the top of the Most Wanted War Criminal list. Still, no one could find him. He had vanished. After a few years, most people stopped looking. But Jewish investigators never gave up. From 1945 on, they continued their search. In 1948 Jews created their own nation, called Israel. The Israeli police sent secret agents around the world

looking for Eichmann. For many years, they had no luck. Then in 1960 they got a break. Someone looking just like Eichmann was spotted in South America.

7   Israel sent secret agents to Buenos Aires, the capital of Argentina. They tracked down the man in question. It was Eichmann! He was living under the name Ricardo Clement and working in a local auto plant. The agents were eager to grab him. They wanted to take him to Israel to stand trial for his war crimes. But they had to be careful. If Eichmann realized they were on his trail, he might disappear again. Then they would have to start the search all over.

8   There was one other problem. Israel had no treaty with Argentina about turning over war criminals. So Argentine police could not be counted on to help the Israeli agents. In fact, the police might try to protect Eichmann. The Israelis decided they would have to kidnap Eichmann. Then somehow they would smuggle him out of the country.

9   On May 11, 1960, the agents set their trap. They followed Eichmann as

he left work. As he walked down the street, a car pulled up beside him and suddenly stopped. Four men jumped out. Eichmann saw them and started to scream. But one of the agents clubbed him over the head. The agents tossed the unconscious Eichmann into the back seat of the car, and the car sped away. The agents then sent a secret message back to Israel: "The beast is in chains."

10   The agents took Eichmann to a hideout a few miles from Buenos Aires. Eichmann thought they were going to murder him on the spot. "Don't kill me!" he begged. "Please don't kill me!" But the agents had no intention of killing Eichmann. Instead, on May 19, they slipped him onto a chartered plane and took off for Israel.

11   Eichmann's trial began on April 11, 1961. It lasted several months. During the trial, Eichmann was kept in a bulletproof glass cage in the courtroom. The Israelis put him there to keep him alive. They didn't want anyone to shoot him before the trial was over.

12   Hundreds of witnesses were called. Many were Jews who had survived Eichmann's death camps. Still, Eichmann maintained he was not guilty. He argued that he had not personally killed anyone. He had simply arranged to send Jews to the camps. It was not his fault, he said, that they had been killed there. Besides, he protested, he was simply following orders. Wasn't that what good soldiers were supposed to do?

13   No one accepted these excuses. The whole world knew what Adolf Eichmann had done. On December 15, 1961, the court announced its verdict. Eichmann, his face pale and twitchy, rose to hear the words of Judge Moshe Landau: "The court finds you guilty."

14   The court convicted Eichmann of war crimes. It also found him guilty of crimes against humanity and crimes against the Jewish people. The judges rejected Eichmann's claim that he was just following orders. As Judge Landau said, Eichmann was not "a puppet in the hands of others. He was among those who pulled the strings. This block of ice . . . this block of marble . . . closed his ears to the voice of his conscience."

15   Judge Landau asked Eichmann if he had anything to say. In Eichmann's final statement, he said, "I am not the monster I am made out to be."

16   The court—and the world— disagreed. Judges sentenced Adolf Eichmann to be hanged. The sentence was carried out on May 31, 1962. The man who had once claimed to be the "World's Number One Jew Killer" had finally been brought to justice.

If you have been timed while reading this article, enter your reading time below. Then turn to the Words-per-Minute Table on page 147 and look up your reading speed (words per minute). Enter your reading speed on the graph on page 148.

Reading Time: Lesson 14

_____ : _____
Minutes   Seconds

A Finding the Main Idea

One statement below expresses the main idea of the article. One statement is too general, or too broad. The other statement explains only part of the article; it is too narrow. Label the statements using the following key:

M—Main Idea   B—Too Broad   N—Too Narrow

_____ 1. The crimes committed during World War II will never be forgotten.

_____ 2. Adolf Eichmann argued that he had not personally killed any Jews and so he was innocent.

_____ 3. Nazi war criminal Adolf Eichmann learned that there was no escape from justice.

_____ Score 15 points for a correct M answer.

_____ Score 5 points for each correct B or N answer.

_____ **Total Score:** Finding the Main Idea

B Recalling Facts

How well do you remember the facts in the article? Put an X in the box next to the answer that correctly completes each statement about the article.

1. Adolf Eichmann was in charge of
   - ☐ a. Germany's labor department.
   - ☐ b. protecting Adolf Hitler from attack.
   - ☐ c. getting rid of Jews.

2. The war in Europe ended when Hitler and the Nazis were defeated in
   - ☐ a. 1945.
   - ☐ b. 1948.
   - ☐ c. 1960.

3. In 1960, Israeli agents found Eichmann living in
   - ☐ a. Germany.
   - ☐ b. Argentina.
   - ☐ c. Israel.

4. Israeli agents captured Eichmann by
   - ☐ a. pulling him into a car as he walked down the street.
   - ☐ b. having the police arrest him at work.
   - ☐ c. surprising him in his home.

5. Israelis protected Eichmann during his trial by
   - ☐ a. giving him a bulletproof vest to wear.
   - ☐ b. putting him in a bulletproof glass cage.
   - ☐ c. not letting him attend the trial.

Score 5 points for each correct answer.

_____ **Total Score:** Recalling Facts

C Making Inferences

When you combine your own experience and information from a text to draw a conclusion that is not directly stated in that text, you are making an inference. Below are five statements that may or may not be inferences based on information in the article. Label the statements using the following key:

C—Correct Inference   **F—Faulty Inference**

_____ 1. Even during a war, soldiers must follow basic laws of morality.

_____ 2. In the eyes of the Israeli judges, the most important thing for a soldier to do is follow orders.

_____ 3. Adolf Eichmann probably felt deep sorrow and pity for Jews during the war.

_____ 4. Many former Nazis in hiding became nervous about their own safety after Eichmann was arrested and tried.

_____ 5. By 1961 most Jews had forgiven and forgotten the way the Nazis had treated the Jewish people.

Score 5 points for each correct answer.

_____ **Total Score:** Making Inferences

D Using Words Precisely

Each numbered sentence below contains an underlined word or phrase from the article. Following the sentence are three definitions. One definition is closest to the meaning of the underlined word. One definition is opposite or nearly opposite. Label those two definitions using the following key; do not label the remaining definition.

C—Closest   **O—Opposite or Nearly Opposite**

1. The Nazis were led by Adolf Hitler, a <u>vile</u> madman.

_____ a. evil

_____ b. eager

_____ c. good

2. Most frightening of all is the fact that, in his own <u>warped</u> mind, Eichmann thought he was right.

_____ a. intelligent

_____ b. healthy

_____ c. twisted

3. The old, the young, and the sick were sent <u>directly</u> to gas chambers.

_____ a. sadly

_____ b. straight

_____ c. after a long delay

4. He had <u>disguised</u> himself in a uniform stolen from a dead German soldier.

_____ a. showed his true identity

_____ b. covered up his identity

_____ c. brought glory to himself

5. Besides, he <u>protested</u>, he was simply following orders.

_____ a. agreed

_____ b. laughed

_____ c. objected

_____ Score 3 points for each correct C answer.

_____ Score 2 points for each correct O answer.

_____ **Total Score:** Using Words Precisely

Enter the four total scores in the spaces below, and add them together to find your Reading Comprehension Score. Then record your score on the graph on page 149.

Score	Question Type	Lesson 14
_____	Finding the Main Idea	
_____	Recalling Facts	
_____	Making Inferences	
_____	Using Words Precisely	
_____	**Reading Comprehension Score**	

Author's Approach

Put an X in the box next to the correct answer.

1. What is the authors' purpose in writing "A Nazi War Criminal"?

☐ a. to express an opinion about the evils of war

☐ b. to inform the reader about a man who committed terrible crimes during a war and was later captured and punished

☐ c. to emphasize the similarities between Adolf Eichmann and Adolf Hitler

2. Which of the following statements from the article best describes the crimes that Adolf Eichmann committed during World War II?

☐ a. Eichmann carried out his hateful work from 1938 to 1945.

☐ b. [Eichmann] was living under the name Ricardo Clement and working in a local auto plant.

☐ c. By 1945 Adolf Eichmann and his henchmen had murdered 6 million Jews.

3. Judging by statements from the article "A Nazi War Criminal," you can conclude that the authors want the reader to think that

☐ a. Eichmann deserved to be punished for his crimes.

☐ b. Eichmann was just being a good soldier and should not have been punished for his actions.

☐ c. Eichmann had no control over the crimes that were committed by the Nazi party against Jews.

_____ Number of correct answers

Record your personal assessment of your work on the Critical Thinking Chart on page 150.

Summarizing and Paraphrasing

Follow the directions provided for question 1. Put an X in the box next to the correct answer for the other questions.

1. Look for the important ideas and events in paragraphs 9 and 10. Summarize those paragraphs in one or two sentences.

_____

_____

_____

_____

2. Below are summaries of the article. Choose the summary that says all the most important things about the article but in the fewest words.

☐ a. Adolf Eichmann was a German leader during World War II. He ordered the deaths of 6 million Jews and then disappeared at the end of the war. Later, he was found, captured, tried, and hanged for his crimes.

☐ b. During World War II, Adolf Eichmann rounded up Jews and put them in concentration camps. He was found years later in Argentina and was brought back to Israel to be put on trial.

☐ c. Investigators searched for years to find Adolf Eichmann, who was a leader in the Nazi party. They found him in Argentina where he was working in an auto plant and took him back to Israel. He died in 1962.

3. Choose the best one-sentence paraphrase for the following sentence from the article: "The agents tossed the unconscious Eichmann into the back seat of the car, and the car sped away."

☐ a. While the agents knocked Eichmann unconscious in the back seat of the car, the driver sped away.

☐ b. After the agents knocked Eichmann unconscious, they tossed him in the back seat of a car, and then the car sped away.

☐ c. The speeding car knocked Eichmann unconscious, and then the agents threw him in the back seat and drove away.

_____ Number of correct answers

Record your personal assessment of your work on the Critical Thinking Chart on page 150.

Critical Thinking

Follow the directions provided for questions 1, 3, 4, and 5. Put an X in the box next to the correct answer for question 2.

1. For each statement below, write O if it expresses an opinion or write F if it expresses a fact.

_____ a. Israeli agents found Eichmann in Argentina in 1960.

_____ b. Adolf Eichmann enjoyed his work.

_____ c. Soldiers must always follow orders, even when the orders are evil.

2. From what the article told about Argentina's feelings about turning over war criminals, you can predict that when the Israeli agents kidnapped Eichmann, Argentina

☐ a. gave them an award.

☐ b. was glad that someone had finally removed Eichmann from the country.

☐ c. was angry with Israel and protested the kidnapping.

3. Choose from the letters below to correctly complete the following statement. Write the letters on the lines.

In the article, _____ and _____ were alike in their attitude toward Jews.

a. Adolf Eichmann

b. Adolf Hitler

c. Judge Moshe Landau

4. Reread paragraph 5. Then choose from the letters below to correctly complete the following statement. Write the letters on the lines.

According to paragraph 5, _____ because _____.

a. Eichmann was captured soon after the war

b. no one recognized Eichmann when he was first captured

c. Eichmann was dressed in the uniform of a dead German soldier

5. In which paragraph did you find your information or details to answer question 2? _____

_____ Number of correct answers

Record your personal assessment of your work on the Critical Thinking Chart on page 150.

Personal Response

If I were the author, I would change _____

_____

_____

because _____

_____

_____

_____

Self-Assessment

Before reading this article, I already knew _____

_____

_____

_____

The Mad Bomber

This cabin in Montana was the workshop in which the "Unabomber," former mathematics professor Ted Kaczynski, assembled package bombs. Kaczynski eluded authorities for years while he sent and personally delivered his deadly mail.

Percy Wood was at his home in Lake Forest, Illinois, when an odd package arrived in the mail. According to the return address, it came from someone named "Enoch Fisher." Wood, who was the president of United Airlines, did not know anyone by that name. But several days earlier he had received a letter with the same return address. The letter had said Wood was about to get an interesting book in the mail. Since this new package was the size and shape of a book, Wood figured that's what it was.

As he opened the package on June 10, 1980, however, it exploded in his hands. The bomb burned not only his hands but his face and a leg as well.

2 It turned out that there was no "Enoch Fisher." The return address led to a deserted lot in Chicago. As authorities investigated the case, they realized the attack was not an isolated act. Rather, it was the work of a serial bomber. Three other bombs had been planted in the Chicago area in the last two years. All bore certain markings that made experts sure they were the work of the same person. But who would do such a thing? And why?

3 Police tried hard to figure out the pattern of the bombings. In each instance the targets had been people linked to universities or airlines. In addition, the bombs all seemed to come from Chicago. Beyond that, there was not much to go on. There was nothing else that tied the victims together.

4 Over the next few years three more bombings took place. Again, the targets were people connected with universities. But these bombs exploded in Utah, Tennessee, and California. Was the bomber on the move? What

was motivating him? And who would be next?

5 By 1985 police had come up with a nickname for the bomber. They called him the "Unabomber" because he seemed so obsessed with universities. But they were really no closer to catching him—or her. The Unabomber had never been seen planting any of the devices.

6 Police believed the Unabomber was getting better at building bombs. They were right. On December 11, 1985, a man named Hugh Scrutton lost his life to a "Unabomb." As Scrutton stepped out of his California computer store, he saw a block of wood on the ground. He bent down and picked it up. When he did so, it blew up. Shrapnel flew in all directions. Much of the sharp metal pierced Scrutton's chest. Some lodged in his heart, killing him.

7 The Unabomber's next attack came in 1987. A computer repairman saw a canvas bag lying in the parking lot behind his shop in Salt Lake City, Utah. When he picked it up, the bag exploded. Again, shrapnel went flying. But this time the victim was lucky. He was injured, but not killed.

8 There was another bit of luck involved with this attack. This time someone got a glimpse of the Unabomber. A woman happened to be looking out a window just a few yards from the parking lot. She saw a man place the canvas bag on the ground. He was a white man, about 5 feet 10 inches tall, with reddish hair and a mustache. She couldn't see much more than that because he was wearing a hooded sweatshirt and dark sunglasses. But at least it was something. At last the police had some clue as to what the Unabomber looked like.

9 By this time experts had also come up with a psychological profile of the killer. They believed he was intelligent and well educated. They thought he might once have held a teaching job. Perhaps he had been fired. Or perhaps his job had been taken over by a computer. That would explain his anger toward universities and those in the computer field. Police questioned more than 200 suspects who fit the profile. But none turned out to be the Unabomber.

10 For the next six years the Unabomber was silent. Some people

hoped he had been scared off for good. But on June 22, 1993, he showed that he was still out there, as dangerous and heartless as ever. On that day a professor at Yale University got a package in the mail. It was a bomb. Two days later the same thing happened to a professor in San Francisco. Both men were badly injured in the explosions.

11   By 1995 the Unabomber had sent out two more bombs. Both proved deadly. One killed a New Jersey businessman. The other killed a man who was a lobbyist for the timber industry.

12   By this time, there was a $1 million reward for information leading to the Unabomber's arrest and conviction. Police had set up a hotline to gather fresh leads. They also kept combing through past attacks, searching for clues. They noted, for instance, that all the bombings had been related to wood in some way. Some bombs had been encased in wood. Others had been sent to people named Wood or people living on streets with names connected to wood. But what exactly did that signify? Frustratingly, no one knew.

13   Meanwhile, people across the country worried about where the Unabomber might strike next. No one could feel safe with him on the loose. In September 1995 the Unabomber showed just how remorseless he was.

On that day he sent a long letter to the New York Times and the Washington Post. In it he said that he had sent the bombs to show his hatred for society. His goal, he said, was to destroy "the worldwide industrial system." He hoped his bombings would encourage people to rise up and reject modern technology. He didn't care that he had ruined people's lives. In his twisted mind, that was not important.

14   Many people were troubled by the Unabomber's words. But a man named David Kaczynski was downright shocked. David worked at a homeless shelter in New York state. He was a peaceful man who led a quiet life. "After I read the first few pages," David said, "my jaw literally dropped." He recognized many of the phrases that the Unabomber used. They were the same phrases his brother Ted had used in letters to him.

15   David was not close to his brother. Theodore "Ted" Kaczynski lived alone in a small cabin in Montana. The two brothers had not seen each other in years. But David loved Ted. He was horrified to think Ted might be the Unabomber. Still, David knew he had to act. The lives of innocent people were at stake. In early 1996 David contacted the FBI and told them his suspicions.

16   A few weeks later, on April 3, Ted Kaczynski was arrested at his cabin. There

the police found proof that he was indeed the Unabomber. They found journals describing his crimes. They also found parts of new bombs. Kaczynski pleaded guilty to the crimes and was sentenced to life in prison.

17   As it turned out, the police profile of the Unabomber had been right in many ways. He was a white man who had grown up in Chicago. He was bright and well educated. In fact, he had gone to Harvard University. For a while Kaczynski had been an assistant professor of mathematics. But then he dropped out of mainstream life and retreated to the mountains of Montana. There he gardened, rode his bike, and worked with wood. No one could be sure what led Ted Kaczynski to commit his evil crimes. But everyone agreed that the world was a better place with him safely behind bars. ✦

If you have been timed while reading this article, enter your reading time below. Then turn to the Words-per-Minute Table on page 147 and look up your reading speed (words per minute). Enter your reading speed on the graph on page 148.

Reading Time: Lesson 15

_____ : _____
Minutes   Seconds

A · Finding the Main Idea

One statement below expresses the main idea of the article. One statement is too general, or too broad. The other statement explains only part of the article; it is too narrow. Label the statements using the following key:

M—Main Idea   **B—Too Broad**   **N—Too Narrow**

_____ 1. After injuring and killing people with his bombs over a period of several years, the Unabomber was finally captured and jailed.

_____ 2. The Unabomber attacked in such secretive ways that no one could feel safe.

_____ 3. Because the targets of the bombs often were people linked with universities, police decided to call the criminal the "Unabomber."

_____ Score 15 points for a correct M answer.

_____ Score 5 points for each correct B or N answer.

_____ **Total Score:** Finding the Main Idea

B · Recalling Facts

How well do you remember the facts in the article? Put an X in the box next to the answer that correctly completes each statement about the article.

1. The return address on the bomb delivered to Percy Wood led police to
   - ☐ a. Ted Kaczynski's mountain retreat.
   - ☐ b. a vacant lot in Chicago.
   - ☐ c. Harvard University.

2. For years police couldn't capture the Unabomber because
   - ☐ a. no one ever saw him planting his bombs.
   - ☐ b. they didn't give this case much attention.
   - ☐ c. his victims all died.

3. One woman who spotted the Unabomber said he was about
   - ☐ a. 6 feet 5 inches tall, with blond hair.
   - ☐ b. 5 feet 10 inches tall, with brown hair and a beard.
   - ☐ c. 5 feet 10 inches tall, with reddish hair and a mustache.

4. In a letter to newspapers, the Unabomber said that his goal was to
   - ☐ a. destroy the worldwide industrial system.
   - ☐ b. bring down the United States government.
   - ☐ c. destroy all American universities.

5. David Kaczynski thought the Unabomber letters in the newspaper were written by his brother, Ted, because
   - ☐ a. Ted had warned him he was going to send letters to a newspaper.
   - ☐ b. he read the same phrases in the Unabomber's letters as were in letters Ted had sent to him.
   - ☐ c. he knew Ted was smart and felt that only a smart person could write those letters.

Score 5 points for each correct answer.

_____ **Total Score:** Recalling Facts

C | Making Inferences

When you combine your own experience with information from a text to draw a conclusion that is not directly stated in that text, you are making an inference. Below are five statements that may or may not be inferences based on information in the article. Label the statements using the following key:

C—Correct Inference   **F—Faulty Inference**

_____ 1. Ted Kaczynski was smarter than the police who were trying to catch him.

_____ 2. People who leave good jobs and retreat to homes in the mountains should not be trusted.

_____ 3. Newspapers printed the Unabomber's letter.

_____ 4. David Kaczynski probably informed the FBI about his brother so he could receive the $1 million reward.

_____ 5. Anyone who feels hatred for society probably wouldn't mind killing people.

Score 5 points for each correct answer.

_____ **Total Score:** Making Inferences

D | Using Words Precisely

Each numbered sentence below contains an underlined word or phrase from the article. Following the sentence are three definitions. One definition is closest to the meaning of the underlined word. One definition is opposite or nearly opposite. Label those two definitions using the following key; do not label the remaining definition.

C—Closest   **O—Opposite or Nearly Opposite**

1. As authorities investigated the case, they realized the attack was not an isolated act. Rather, it was the work of a <u>serial</u> bomber.

_____ a. sick

_____ b. doing a series of acts one after the other

_____ c. doing an action only once

2. The Unabomber had never been seen <u>planting</u> any of the devices.

_____ a. placing

_____ b. building

_____ c. taking away

3. They also kept <u>combing</u> through past attacks.

_____ a. ignoring

_____ b. looking carefully

_____ c. thinking

4. In September 1995 the Unabomber showed just how <u>remorseless</u> he was.

_____ a. stupid

_____ b. sad and guilty about his actions

_____ c. feeling no guilt or sorrow for his actions

5. But then he dropped out of <u>mainstream</u> life and retreated to the mountains of Montana.

_____ a. normal

_____ b. unusual

_____ c. happy

_____ Score 3 points for each correct C answer.

_____ Score 2 points for each correct O answer.

_____ **Total Score:** Using Words Precisely

Enter the four total scores in the spaces below, and add them together to find your Reading Comprehension Score. Then record your score on the graph on page 149.

Score	Question Type	Lesson 15
_____	Finding the Main Idea	
_____	Recalling Facts	
_____	Making Inferences	
_____	Using Words Precisely	
_____	**Reading Comprehension Score**	

Author's Approach

Put an X in the box next to the correct answer.

1. The main purpose of the first paragraph is to

☐ a. tell the reader who was the president of United Airlines in 1980.

☐ b. describe the package that Percy Wood received.

☐ c. introduce the crime that the article is about.

2. What is the authors' purpose in writing "The Mad Bomber"?

☐ a. to encourage the reader to examine his or her mail carefully

☐ b. to inform the reader about a famous crime

☐ c. to convey a mood of terror

3. From the statements below, choose those that you believe the authors would agree with.

☐ a. David Kaczynski should not have turned in his own brother.

☐ b. David Kaczynski did the right thing when he told the FBI about his suspicions about his brother.

☐ c. David Kaczynski was not happy that he had to inform the FBI about his brother.

4. Choose the statement below that best describes the authors' position in paragraph 13.

☐ a. The Unabomber was both sick and cruel.

☐ b. Although the Unabomber's point of view was worthwhile, his tactics were not effective.

☐ c. The Unabomber was pitiful but he tried hard to do good.

_____ Number of correct answers

Record your personal assessment of your work on the Critical Thinking Chart on page 150.

Summarizing and Paraphrasing

Follow the directions provided for questions 1 and 2. Put an X in the box next to the correct answer for question 3.

1. Complete the following one-sentence summary of the article using the lettered phrases from the phrase bank below. Write the letters on the lines.

> **Phrase Bank**
>
> a. how much destruction the Unabomber caused over several years
> b. the identification and capture of the Unabomber
> c. a description of one bomb sent by the Unabomber

The article "The Mad Bomber" begins with _____, goes on

to explain _____, and ends with _____.

2. Reread paragraph 10 in the article. Below, write a summary of the paragraph in no more than 25 words.

_____

_____

_____

_____

Reread your summary and decide whether it covers the important ideas in the paragraph. Next, decide how to shorten the summary to 15 words or less without leaving out any essential information. Write this summary below.

_____

_____

_____

3. Choose the sentence that correctly restates the following sentence from the article: "She couldn't see much more than that because he was wearing a hooded sweatshirt and dark sunglasses."

☐ a. Because she was wearing a hooded sweatshirt and dark sunglasses, she had trouble seeing much more.

☐ b. The man's hooded sweatshirt and dark sunglasses prevented her from seeing much more.

☐ c. She saw much more than that but could only remember his hooded sweatshirt and dark sunglasses.

> _____ Number of correct answers
>
> Record your personal assessment of your work on the Critical Thinking Chart on page 150.

Critical Thinking

Follow the directions provided for the following questions.

1. For each statement below, write O if it expresses an opinion or write F if it expresses a fact.

_____ a. The Unabomber chose a poor way to get his point across.

_____ b. No opinion or belief is worth the life of an innocent person.

_____ c. Ted Kaczynski wanted others to reject modern technology, just as he had.

2. Choose from the letters below to correctly complete the following statement. Write the letters on the lines.

In the article, _____ and _____ are different.

a. the fate of a New Jersey businessman who received a bomb

b. the fate of the airline president who received a bomb

c. the fate of a timber industry lobbyist who received a bomb

3. Choose from the letters below to correctly complete the following statement. Write the letters on the lines.

According to the article, _____ caused David Kaczynski to

_____, and the effect was _____.

a. the FBI arrested Ted Kaczynski a few weeks later

b. report the similarities to the FBI

c. familiar phrases in the Unabomber's letters

4. Which paragraphs from the article provide evidence that

supports your answer to question 3? _____

_____ Number of correct answers

Record your personal assessment of your work on the Critical Thinking Chart on page 150.

Personal Response

What was most surprising or interesting to you about this article?

_____

_____

_____

Self-Assessment

The part I found most difficult about the article was _____

_____

_____

I found this difficult because _____

_____

_____

_____

Compare and Contrast

Pick three criminals you read about in Unit Three. Write the titles of the articles that tell about them in the first column of the chart below. Use the information you learned from the articles to fill in the empty boxes in the chart.

Title	Why might the criminal have committed his or her crime?	Who was hurt by the crimes?	What punishment was given to each criminal?

The punishment I would suggest for the criminal _____ would be _____

I think that is a proper punishment because _____

_____

_____

Words-per-Minute Table

Unit Three

Directions: If you were timed while reading an article, refer to the Reading Time you recorded in the box at the end of the article. Use this words-per-minute table to determine your reading speed for that article. Then plot your reading speed on the graph on page 148.

Lesson / No. of Words	11 / 933	12 / 1,049	13 / 1,036	14 / 1,082	15 / 1,263	Seconds
1:30	622	699	691	721	842	90
1:40	560	629	622	649	758	100
1:50	509	572	565	590	689	110
2:00	467	525	518	541	632	120
2:10	431	484	478	499	583	130
2:20	400	450	444	464	541	140
2:30	373	420	414	433	505	150
2:40	350	393	389	406	474	160
2:50	329	370	366	382	446	170
3:00	311	350	345	361	421	180
3:10	295	331	327	342	399	190
3:20	280	315	311	325	379	200
3:30	267	300	296	309	361	210
3:40	254	286	283	295	344	220
3:50	243	274	270	282	329	230
4:00	233	262	259	271	316	240
4:10	224	252	249	260	303	250
4:20	215	242	239	250	291	260
4:30	207	233	230	240	281	270
4:40	200	225	222	232	271	280
4:50	193	217	214	224	261	290
5:00	187	210	207	216	253	300
5:10	181	203	201	209	244	310
5:20	175	197	194	203	237	320
5:30	170	191	188	721	230	330
5:40	165	185	183	191	223	340
5:50	160	180	178	185	217	350
6:00	156	175	173	180	211	360
6:10	151	170	168	175	205	370
6:20	147	166	164	649	199	380
6:30	144	161	159	166	194	390
6:40	140	157	155	162	189	400
6:50	137	154	152	158	185	410
7:00	133	150	148	155	180	420
7:10	130	146	145	151	176	430
7:20	127	143	141	148	172	440
7:30	124	140	138	144	168	450
7:40	122	137	135	141	165	460
7:50	119	134	132	138	161	470
8:00	117	131	130	135	158	480

Minutes and Seconds

Plotting Your Progress: Reading Speed

Unit Three

Directions: If you were timed while reading an article, write your words-per-minute rate for that article in the box under the number of the lesson. Then plot your reading speed on the graph by putting a small X on the line directly above the number of the lesson, across from the number of words per minute you read. As you mark your speed for each lesson, graph your progress by drawing a line to connect the X's.

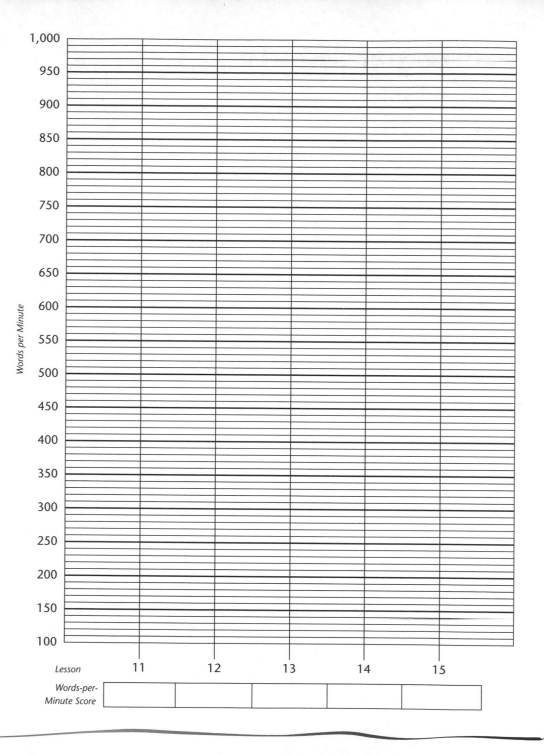

Plotting Your Progress: Reading Comprehension

Unit Three

Directions: Write your Reading Comprehension score for each lesson in the box under the number of the lesson. Then plot your score on the graph by putting a small X on the line directly above the number of the lesson and across from the score you earned. As you mark your score for each lesson, graph your progress by drawing a line to connect the X's.

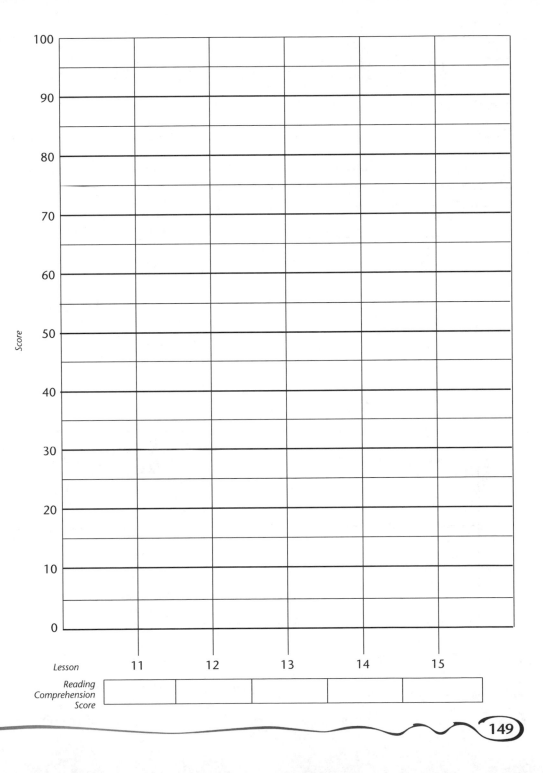

Plotting Your Progress: Critical Thinking

Unit Three

Directions: Work with your teacher to evaluate your responses to the Critical Thinking questions for each lesson. Then fill in the appropriate spaces in the chart below. For each lesson and each type of Critical Thinking question, do the following: Mark a minus sign (–) in the box to indicate areas in which you feel you could improve. Mark a plus sign (+) to indicate areas in which you feel you did well. Mark a minus-slash-plus sign (–/+) to indicate areas in which you had mixed success. Then write any comments you have about your performance, including ideas for improvement.

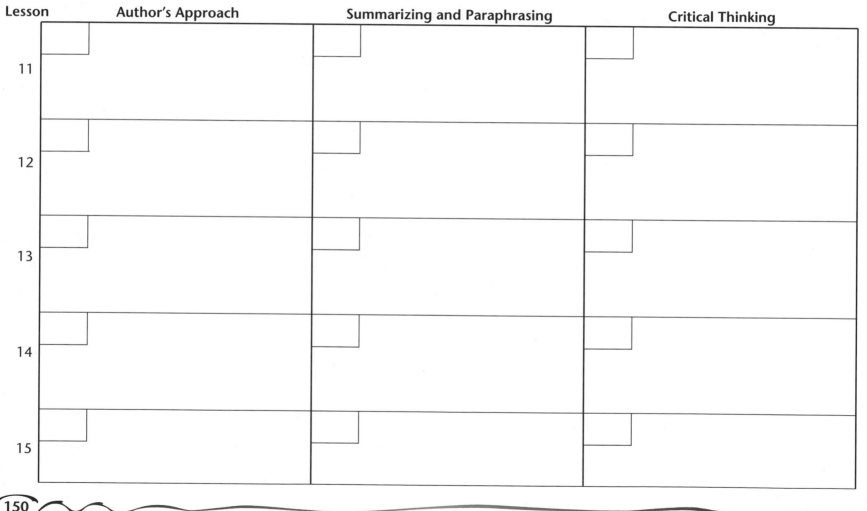

Lesson	Author's Approach	Summarizing and Paraphrasing	Critical Thinking
11			
12			
13			
14			
15			

Photo Credits